Heroic efforts don't always take place on battlefields. What John and Stacey Holley have done to restore dignity and honor for our fallen warriors deserves more than a medal or a few headlines, it merits our nation's eternal gratitude.

— **SALVADOR RIVERA**, Former KGTV-ABC 10 News Reporter

General Douglas MacArthur made famous the saying, *"Old soldiers never die, they just fade away."* John and Stacey Holley are by no means 'old' soldiers — but soldiers and warriors they are! And they did not fade away. When their son returned home, having sustained mortal wounds on a combat mission in Iraq, they were mystified, horrified, and indignant over the way returning heroes were being handled. Thus began their crusade, not just for Matthew, but also for every other American hero who has defended freedom and done so with his or her life. This is their story.

In that same speech to Congress, General MacArthur also said, *"In war there is no substitute for victory."* John and Stacey were victorious in their battle – the benefits of which serve every fallen hero who returns home as did their son. More importantly it's a respectful and lasting memory offered the loved ones of that fallen hero, as the last measure of devotion on behalf of a grateful nation. I have watched them through this horrible time. I have tried to understand their loss, comfort them in their sorrow, and catch their tears. In all of this I have admired their strength and resolve.

This book is about courage, integrity, and honor. I invite you to share John and Stacey's journey. It is a trip you will not soon forget.

— **PASTOR JIM W. BAIZE**, Ocean View Church, San Diego, CA

When their only son, Matthew, was killed by a roadside bomb in Iraq, John and Stacey Holley tumbled into the utter depths of despair. This book is the extraordinary story of their search for healing and understanding. A must-read for every American family with loved ones in the military.

— **JEFF EDWARDS**, Award winning author of *SEA OF SHADOWS* and *THE SEVENTH ANGEL*

Medals, Flags and Memories

Medals, Flags and Memories

The Storm of Our Lives
A Story of Courage, Faith and Honor

John and Stacey Holley

NAVIGATOR BOOKS

MEDALS, FLAGS AND MEMORIES

Copyright © 2011 by John and Stacey Holley

Navigator Books

www.navigator-books.com

Paperback cover design adapted from the first edition hardback, published by SP Press. Hardback edition cover art concept by John Holley, layout by Dana Wascher, DW Graphx — DWGraphx.com.

Biblical references taken from the HOLY BIBLE, New International Version®. Copyright 1973, 1978, and 1984 by International Bible Society. Used by permission of Zondervan Publishing House. All rights reserved.

The "NIV" and "New International Version" trademarks are registered in the United States Patent and Trademark Office by International Bible Society. Use of either trademark requires the permission of International Bible Society.

ISBN-13: 978-0-9834168-2-1

Printed in the United States of America

Dedicated to:

The Glory of Our Lord and Savior
Our Family and Friends
In Memory of America's Fallen Heroes

And

To those who continue to serve our nation selflessly

Matthew's Prayer

"I actually had some time to think today about what's coming up around the blind corner called my future. I'm going into the U.S. Army to be a Medic. Combat Medic more exactly, they just don't call it that any more. I've always wanted to help people so this is that "it's my chance" kind of thing... So I'll do my best...

If you're religious or believe in God then pray this with me, and if you're not you can read along...

Lord, some things in life are unrevealed. Some things are never to be known. Show me, guide me. It's through faith that I'll know; through your love that I'll become. Protect what I love and I thank you for the blessings and gifts bestowed on me even if they are unrevealed to me... Amen"

Matthew John Holley – January 17, 2004

Table of Contents

Author's Note

The story of Matthew John Holley began in September 1984, in the small North Idaho town of Post Falls. It ended in Taji, Iraq, on November 15, 2005, at the hands of murderers.

That fateful day Matthew and others in his patrol were returning to their camp when the Humvee they were riding in rolled over an Improvised Explosive Device (IED). From what little information has been provided to us, the Humvee was destroyed beyond recognition. Matthew and three others inside either perished immediately, shortly after the blast, or within 24 hours of the attack. We would learn later that there was one survivor that day.

In short, this could be considered the beginning and end of this story. A young person who answered a call to duty, honor and country and in the end gave his life for something greater than himself. Matthew, or Matt as he preferred to be called, was not unlike so many other young men and women in today's America. Many who are searching for their place, their direction and even to some extent themselves. Not choosing to continue his education directly after high school, seeking instead to explore adventure, Matt joined the United States Army. After considering several options he decided — based on his desire to help others — that he wanted to be an Army Combat Medic. As his parents, we would have preferred anything other than combat military service. However, in an effort to let go as all parents need to do at some point, we honored his wishes. It was with fear, sadness and trepidation that in February 2004 we let our son and only child leave our home to pursue his future. Many have told us that we did the right thing in letting go. However, it's easy to doubt one's decision when you're tasked with the responsibility and finality of laying your only child to rest.

And so this story begins at the end, rather than the beginning. A story of inspiration, hope, faith, sadness, and one of encouragement to parents who wonder if the decisions made in raising their sons or daughters are good enough.

Foreword

In this story of Global War on Terror focused in Iraq and Afghanistan, is a story of families, a story of enormous sacrifice. Not just by people who wear the uniform in the theatre, but by the families back home. There is a particular family, the Holley family from San Diego, California, that brought an issue to the attention of the Committee on Armed Services when their great 101st Airborne trooper, Matthew Holley, was killed in the Iraq theatre...

The Holleys pointed out that in the transportation of our fallen heroes home, when they come through Dover, Delaware, and ultimately go to their final resting place at their particular hometown or community in America — that a part of that transportation has been carried out by commercial airlines. Despite the best wishes and best efforts on the part of the people who operate the commercial airlines, the proper amount of respect, the extreme amount of respect, that should be afforded these fallen heroes has in some cases been lacking. This came to the attention of the Holley Family, and they talked to me and other members of the Committee, and we looked at the issue.

As a result of that, the law of "The Holley Provision" includes some very clear and strong directives to the Administration: to utilize military aircraft in taking our fallen heroes from Dover, Delaware - where they land on our shores - to the military base closest to their hometown, unless otherwise directed by the family, and to use these military aircraft to accompany those fallen heroes with American military personnel, and to greet that military aircraft when it arrives at that military base closest to their hometown with an honor guard.

I want to thank John and Stacey Holley who really brought this to our attention in honor of their son Matthew Holley.

— Congressman Duncan Hunter (Ret), Chairman of the Committee on Armed Services

(Entered into the Congressional Record May 10, 2006)

The Doorbell

THERE ARE CERTAIN SOUNDS that no rational person ever wants to hear — the screeching of brakes... the shattering of glass... a cry of pain. These noises are unwelcome reminders that human beings are frail creatures, and that our safety can be threatened without warning. The sound of approaching sirens or the sudden blare of a car horn proclaim loudly that we cannot always protect the people we love. They force us to confront the knowledge that our spouses, our children, and our friends are all vulnerable to the sudden whims of fate.

We don't dwell on such dark ideas most of the time. We're too busy living our lives to think about all the things that can possibly go wrong. Then our ears catch some noise that brings our inner fears rushing back to the surface.

For most people, the trigger sounds are limited to obvious signals of danger. The sound of distant gunshots or the metallic crunch of colliding vehicles is enough to quicken anyone's pulse. But for the loved ones of deployed active duty military personnel, there is another sound that's more frightening than any siren or gunshot. It's the sound of the doorbell. How many times in our lives do we hear the ringing of a doorbell? With tones, buzzes, or chimes they signal the arrival of neighbors, friends and family members — loved ones, strangers and salespeople. They announce the delivery of packages, and alert us to the presence of candy-seeking goblins and superheroes every Halloween night.

Doorbells can be soft or loud, gentle or harsh. They can be as different as the people who own them, as varied as the homes they guard. But all doorbells have one thing in common: they do not reveal the nature of the visitors they announce. The ringing of the bell tells us only that someone is standing at our door. It offers us no clue who that someone might be, or what business brings them to our home. So the ringing of our doorbell on November 16, 2005 gave no warning at all. The sound should have split the cool autumn air like a crack of thunder. The weight of its message should have rattled our house in North Idaho to its very foundation. Instead, the doorbell sounded exactly the same as it always had. The two simple tones offered no clue to us that our lives were about to come crashing down around us.

John:

I had talked about the doorbell before. With our son Matthew serving in Iraq, sometimes I couldn't bear the thought of answering the door. What would I do if some uniformed stranger showed up on our front step bearing the worst possible news? What could *anyone* do in such a situation?

I was in my home office that afternoon, chatting with a young service technician who was doing some work on our computers. We were leafing through one of Matthew's sketchbooks, admiring his artwork, when the technician spotted a martial arts statue on one of the bookshelves.

"Matt's into karate," I said. "That's his 2003 U.S. AAU National Champion Black Belt trophy for eighteen year-olds." I found it hard to keep the pride out of my voice.

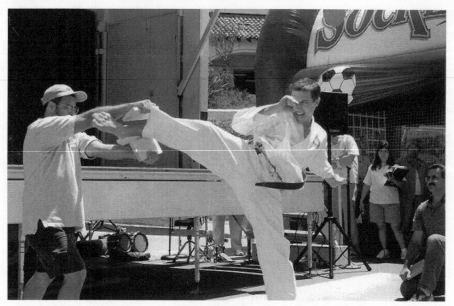

Matthew demonstrating his love of the martial arts. His efforts led to three national titles, including the U.S. AAU National 18 year-old Black Belt championship in 2003.

The young technician smiled and replied, "I used to study martial arts; in fact, I'm taking lessons again."

I recognized an opportunity to do two things I loved: encourage young people, and brag about my son. I opened my mouth to say something encouraging, but was interrupted by the doorbell.

"Hold that thought," I said. "I'll be right back."

With Matt's sketchbook still in my hand, I went to answer the door.

The office was only a few yards down the hall from the living room. Simple math tells me that I must have covered the distance in a matter of seconds. But when the memories of that day come flooding back, those few short yards of floor become the longest and most difficult miles I ever walked.

I was near the top of the stairs leading down from the living room to the entrance, when I spotted a pair of uniformed figures through the little window in the door. I caught a quick glimpse of medals, and the flash of some sort of insignia. I wondered what the police were doing on our doorstep when the doorbell shattered the silence again.

The realization crashed over me in a sickening wave. These were not police officers. They were military personnel. I reached the bottom of the stairs and put my hand on the doorknob, but I didn't open the door. Perhaps if I didn't allow these uniformed strangers into our home, they would simply go away. And if they went away, maybe their dreadful news would go with them. Maybe it wouldn't be true.

It took an act of nearly supreme will, but I managed to force myself to open the door.

There were two of them, a U.S. Army First Sergeant, and an Air Force Major with the collar devices of a military chaplain. They stood without speaking, bathed in the cool clear Idaho sunlight, too weighed down by the burden of their terrible message to utter a word.

The sight of their solemn faces hit me like a punch in the chest. "No!" My voice was practically a scream. "No, no! *Please* don't tell me!"

Before either man could speak, I felt a faint stirring of hope. "Wait a minute," I said.

"Matt's just wounded, right? Please tell me he's just wounded."

The sergeant shook his head slowly. "I'm sorry, sir. I am so sorry."

The world seemed to blur. I felt my body sag against the doorframe, and I heard a man's voice, drawn out into a groan of unearthly despair. I was vaguely aware that it was my own voice, the sound of my very soul constricting painfully in my chest. The sketchbook dropped from my hand, Matt's drawings fluttered to the ground like autumn leaves.

The two military men watched in silence as I began to cry.

I felt a tiny flicker of pride and defiance. I straightened my backbone, pushed away from the doorframe and drew myself up to a full standing position. "You've just killed me," I said. "You know, you've just killed me."

I jerked my arm to motion the two strangers into the house towards the living room.

When they stepped past me onto the stairs, I knelt down and began to retrieve Matthew's beautiful drawings from the floor.

By the time I reached the top of the stairs, I had regained some of my composure. I sat down opposite the two military men. "Tell me what happened," I said softly.

The sergeant unfolded a piece of paper, and began to read from a prepared statement. His hands were trembling, and so was his voice. "The President of the United States regrets to inform you…"

The words seared themselves into my brain. The President of the United States wanted to inform us that our son was gone. Our boy, our young man, our beloved Matthew. The child we had raised, guided, and protected for nearly twenty-one years, had been killed by an improvised explosive device on the 15th of November, at approximately 5:15 p.m. Iraq time.

There was little else the gentlemen sharing this horrific news could tell me, because that was all they knew. This was the first time either of the men had been called to perform notification duty, and I could see that it wasn't much easier on them than it was on me. Their eyes were just as blurred with tears as mine.

After several minutes, the sergeant wiped his eyes with the back of his hand. "What time is your wife due home, sir?"

"She's at work," I responded. "She usually calls me around 5:30 to let me know she's on her way home."

The sergeant nodded gravely. "Do you want us to wait with you, sir?"

"Yes." My voice was nearly a whisper. "I think that would be best."

The next fifteen minutes stretched into an eternity of painful silence, broken only by the rhythmic ticking of the clock. No one felt like talking. None of us had any idea what to say. But as awkward as the silence was, I was grateful for the presence of the two strangers. I didn't want to be alone.

That thought struck a chord in my head. I hadn't been alone. I'd been with the computer technician. I'd forgotten the poor man entirely.

I stood up. "I'll be right back."

As I walked down the hall toward the office, it occurred to me that I'd said those exact words to the technician. "I'll be right back." But I hadn't come right back. I *hadn't* come back at all. My quick trip down the living room stairs had not taken me to the front door. It had taken me into the world of darkness and grief that existed on the other side of the ringing doorbell. A world from which I felt I might never return.

The technician was putting on his coat when I reached the office. His young face was pale, and he was visibly shaken. I could tell instantly that he had overheard everything, and that he was preparing to leave quietly, perhaps to avoid intruding at our family's moment of grief.

"Please don't go," I uttered. "I need you to stay and finish the job. We're going to..." I stopped and swallowed, struggling to go on. "We're going to need these computers more than ever now."

The technician nodded and removed his coat. He was already working on the computers again when I left the room.

I returned to the living room, dropped into my seat on the couch, and the three of us resumed our silent vigil. It was almost 5:30. The phone was going to ring soon. Stacey would be calling any minute.

What would I say? What *could* I say? My brain was numb. I couldn't give her the news over the phone; that much I knew. I needed to wait and tell her in person.

But what was I going to say? Could I make myself go through the motions of an ordinary phone call? Could I fake business-as-usual for the few minutes it would take to get her off the phone?

I had to. Somehow — I didn't know how — I had to do it.

The phone rang right on time.

The sergeant looked up. "Would you like me to answer that?"

"No. I'll do it."

I reached for the receiver. My body seemed to be on autopilot now, muscles moving, heart pumping, fingers working, all of their own accord. The phone was like a dead weight in my hand. The only spark of reality came from Stacey's voice, alive with excitement as she chatted about the trip we were planning to take in a couple of days. We were going to the coast to celebrate Thanksgiving with family at the home of Stacey's parents.

The very concept seemed completely alien now. *Thanksgiving — Celebration*? How could we ever celebrate again? What was left to be thankful for?

The ticking of the clock seemed even louder, announcing each new second that passed in this strange and monstrous world — this unfathomable place that had no Matthew in it.

I nearly choked. I gripped the telephone so tightly that my fingers ached. "I love you," I said. I wanted to scream, but I kept my voice as gentle as I could manage. "I'll see you in a little while."

I hung up the phone.

"You handled that pretty well," the chaplain said.

I didn't answer. As difficult as it had been, the phone call was the easy part. Now I had to find the strength to tell my wife that our only child was gone.

I recall fumbling silently for the right words, and not finding them. I was still racking my brain some unknowable time later, when the rumble of the garage door announced Stacey's arrival.

I stood up. My legs seemed as unresponsive as wood, but they managed to carry me into the garage. I still had no idea what I was going to say, but I knew that I had to go to her. I didn't know why, but it suddenly seemed important to meet her before she came into the house.

Stacey was climbing out of the car when I entered the garage. The second we made eye contact, I began to cry again.

Alarm sprang into her eyes. "What's wrong?"

The magic words did not come. There was no perfect phrase that would deliver the news gently and gracefully. "Matthew has gone to heaven." They weren't the words I had hoped for, but they were the only ones I could find.

Stacey's face went from shock to disbelief in an instant.

"What?"

"Matthew has gone to heaven," I sobbed.

And then Stacey was crying too, reaching to put her arms around me.

My tears came even harder. "*Please* don't hate me." I don't know why I said those words, or what they meant, but I found myself repeating them. "Please don't hate me."

Stacey's arms tightened around me. "I don't hate you! Why would I hate you?" She looked toward the door leading to the house. "Are they in there?" She seemed to know instinctively that the messengers of this terrible news were still in the house.

I nodded.

We walked into the house together and sat side by side on the couch.

Stacey looked from the chaplain, to the sergeant, and back to the chaplain. And then she began to ask questions — the same questions I had asked just minutes before. And she learned what I already knew. The messengers knew almost nothing of Matthew's death. They had no details to share. There *were* no answers.

Next Steps

Stacey:

The sergeant began to outline the next steps in our family's journey. He asked us to sign a few documents, primarily acknowledgement forms. He informed us that there would be a lot more paperwork later, but these were enough to get the process moving. He told us to expect a visit from another sergeant on the following day. The new sergeant would be assigned as our Casualty Assistance Officer, and he would bring more information and more paperwork.

At last, the formalities were over. The sergeant and the chaplain rose to leave. They offered their condolences again, and the chaplain asked us to pray with him. After a short prayer we led the two gentlemen out into the crisp night. As their car disappeared into the darkness, we stood clinging to each other in a state of emotional paralysis. What were we supposed to do next?

The young man from the computer store was still inside, working on our computers. We made our way back to the living room, and sat in stunned silence for nearly two hours while he finished his work.

At last he was done, and John led him to the door. As John signed the technician's work order, the young man again expressed his condolences, and John acknowledged him with a nod. "Call your parents, and tell them you love them." His voice was husky with emotion. "In fact, make it a habit to do that every day. You never know when something is going to happen and you may not have that chance."

That was one bit of comfort, at least. We had always made it a point to tell Matthew that we loved him, from the day he was born until our last conversation with him just five days earlier. We might have other things to regret, but we will never have any regrets about that.

When the door closed behind the technician, it was time to start discussing our next steps. Someone had to break the news to our family and friends. John didn't think he could do it. He couldn't bear to repeat over and over again that Matthew had gone to heaven.

9

And so it was with a heavy heart that I began making the calls.

The first step in that process was the simplest, and yet the most difficult — picking up the telephone. The phone had always been a tool of convenience, a personal connection. It had suddenly become the conduit for the worst news that I would ever have to deliver.

I decided to begin with our closest of friends, Matthew's godparents, Mark and Louise Johnsen who lived just a short distance from our Idaho home, and Stephen and Rebecca Meyer who were in San Diego.

If you are fortunate, there are people you learn that you can rely on in life. If you're truly blessed, some of them will be people you can implicitly trust to provide advice and spiritual guidance to your children if the unthinkable should befall you. We chose Matthew's godparents with that in mind, knowing that they would gladly share their love and their wisdom with Matthew in our absence.

With the diligence of loving mothers and fathers everywhere, we had prepared for Matthew's continued life after our own deaths. What we had not prepared for was our own lives after the death of our son.

I picked up the receiver and began to dial the Johnsen's number. A few seconds later, I tearfully explained to Louise that our child — the one we had entrusted to them — had gone home to be with his Lord.

The pain flowed through the telephone receiver like a palpable force. Matthew's beloved godparents were wounded as deeply and profoundly as we were. They had stood alongside us and watched our promising child grow into a man of conviction. And now, without warning, his life on earth as we knew it was over. They knew, as we did, that Matthew wasn't perfect. He had his share of faults, as all of us do. However, when it came to matters of personal belief, Matthew had always stood his ground. He had joined the Army with that principle in mind. His desire to serve our nation had been utterly clear in his words… *To serve a cause greater than himself.*

I made call after call that night, and well into the next morning. There were so many people to tell. Matthew had touched so very many lives. In some cases, I asked friends or family members to make calls on our behalf. I knew that the task would be no easier for them than it was for me.

After a while, the phone began to ring every time I replaced the receiver. As people heard the news, the calls of condolence began flooding in. Everyone was stunned, and they all asked the same questions. What? Where? Why? How?

We were still asking those same questions ourselves, and finding very few answers.

Mark and Louise, who lived just a short distance from us, rushed over as quickly as they could to be there for us and to share in our sorrow. We found ourselves just sitting there. It was impossible to make sense of anything at that point in time.

It's fair to say that at such a time there can be a supreme instance of doubt for any believer, some terrible point in time, when pain and anger can rock your faith in God to its very core. Understanding that there is such a threshold in all persons, ours came that night. There were moments when we could have simply turned away from the Lord. But we didn't. God was there for us in those hours of darkness. We needed Him that first night, and we knew that we would need Him just as deeply in the days, months and even years to come.

John:

As we lay in bed that night, not really sleeping, my heart pounded so hard I thought that it would burst. The pain in my head was so intense that I didn't know if I would make it through till morning.

I began to wonder if I was going to die. And then, I actually started to hope that I would. If I died, the pain would stop. I would be with Matthew again. The nightmare would be over. The pain was unbearable, but the guilt was even worse. I was the dad. I was supposed to protect my son. That's what a father does; he shields his son from the worst the world can dish out. He stands between his son and danger. If necessary, he surrenders his own life to defend his child. But I had not done that. I had not been in Iraq. I had not been there to throw my body on the IED. I had not been there to shield Matthew's body from the blast that had taken his life. And Matthew had faced that final and hideous second without the protection of his father.

The guilt didn't end there. Maybe we hadn't tried hard enough to make Matthew understand the ramifications of choosing a combat rating. We'd supported his decision to serve in the military, but we had not wanted him to serve in a combat role. Had we made that clear enough? Had we failed to impress on him the potential consequences of his decision? Had he not properly understood the danger?

No. That part wasn't true. Matthew had been a three-time national karate champion. He had been fearless. He had known the danger, and he had decided to face it. Anything less would have been beneath him.

Matthew hadn't wanted just any job. He'd decided to become a combat medic. He had known the risks, and he had accepted the challenge. It was a task worthy of heroes. And he had stepped up to the challenge with both eyes open.

The Incident

John:

In those earliest days we had so many questions, and no one seemed to have any real answers. Even now, as the months since Matthew's death have begun to stretch into years, we still don't know much about the events of that fateful day in 2005. So many of our questions are still unanswered.

What little we do know has been pieced together from a discussion I had with the sole survivor of the incident, Private First Class Brian Daniels. Brian recounted his story for me, and it helped to put some of the pieces of the puzzle together. In some cases, we can only surmise what may have happened.

By all accords Brian was a typical nineteen-year-old Soldier — happy, with no real cares in the world. Just going along to get along. That is, until the world exploded in his face on November 15, 2005.

There were five men assigned to ride in that Humvee. Their ages ranged from 19 to 33. Some of them were single, some were married, and some were fathers. They arrived at the Humvee at about 0500 hours, standing around making small talk as they checked their gear and prepared for the mission ahead of them.

We know from Brian that the Soldiers prayed individually — not as a group — for their safety. When the last Amen had been spoken, the five men mounted up for patrol as they had done many times in the past month.

The morning winds off the desert carried no trace of an omen. There was no sign that this day would be any different from the day before.

Private First Class Travis Grigg fired up the engine, and the Humvee rolled out to the team's assigned checkpoint. The Soldiers relieved the off-going teams and began taking turns patrolling their designated zone.

The pattern followed the established routine without a hitch. A pair of Humvees — each containing five Soldiers — would patrol for two or three hours, and then they would trade off with the next team. Brian told me that it was a wonderful day by Iraq standards. "Almost too easy," he said.

The team went to the bazaar for lunch, just like they usually did. They talked about their schedule, getting their patrols completed for the day, their upcoming night periods, and the trip back to the base the following afternoon. Piece of cake! No worries!

Brian relayed that while they were out on the road, they talked about politics, sports, and all the usual stuff, but mostly about their girls. At around 1700 hours — just about dusk — their two-vehicle patrol was winding its way down a stretch of road that they had walked and driven down many times. They felt pretty secure. This was familiar territory. They'd been back and forth across it many times without incident. He described it to me in one word... "Safe."

Matthew on patrol in Iraq, November 2005.

Their Humvee rolled slowly down the road behind the lead vehicle until they reached the turnaround point. As was normal, Matthew's Humvee — in the trailing position — provided cover for the lead Humvee while it pulled off the paved road into a driveway to make a u-turn.

The lead vehicle made the turn safely. Everything looked perfectly normal, so Private First Class Grigg pulled the Humvee off the road into the same driveway, careful to follow the exact path that the first vehicle had navigated safely just a few seconds earlier.

The blast came with no warning at all. One second Matthew and his buddies were calmly looking out the window, and a millisecond later — *Whooooom*! Their vehicle was torn apart in a fury of fire and broken steel.

No one saw the IED. No one had even a split-second of forewarning. The world went to fire and chaos in the space of a single deafening detonation.

The front half of the Humvee was completely obliterated, and all five Soldiers were thrown from the vehicle in different directions.

As Brian recalled the scene for me, he described a view of destruction unlike anything he had ever seen. Sergeant James Estep and Private First Class Grigg were killed instantly. Private First Class Brian Daniels, Specialist Alex Roman-Cruz, and Matthew were still alive. They lay on the ground, dazed and screaming from the pain of their injuries.

The Soldiers from the lead vehicle dismounted immediately and began rendering what aid they could as they called in the Quick Response Team (QRT) to assist.

Initial reports show that Roman-Cruz was severely injured in the thigh and arm, Brian's right foot was nearly severed, and Matthew had suffered severe blunt force trauma to the head.

Sergeant Floyd, one of the first team members on the scene, attended to Matthew. He knelt by Matthew's side and held his hand.

"How do I look?" Matthew asked.

We can only assume that he was asking how severe his injuries were, but we'll never know for certain. Matthew mumbled something, and then he slipped into unconsciousness and passed away.

Sergeant Floyd left Matthew's side to assist with prepping Daniels and Roman-Cruz for evacuation.

Unfortunately, Matthew was the only combat medic for the twenty Soldiers assigned to the four Humvee patrol group. He was the only one present with advanced medical training.

When his life slipped away, all of that knowledge slipped away with it. The remaining Soldiers had to do what little they could until the medivac helicopter arrived.

Brian Daniels lost consciousness somewhere in the process. His next memory is of waking up on the helicopter and asking, "Where's Doc?" He was looking for Matthew, his combat medic. If somebody was going to work on him, he wanted it to be Matthew.

The attending medics told him that Matthew was busy, and couldn't come right now. Then the helicopter lifted off rushing Daniels and Roman-Cruz to the hospital.

Brian told me he learned later that the remainder of the QRT stayed behind at the scene of the incident. They administered the last rites to Matthew and his fallen brothers. Then they zipped them into body bags for transport back to Camp Taji, where the sad process of returning them home to their loved ones would begin.

Roman-Cruz died from his wounds the next day, bringing the death toll to four. Brian Daniels was now the sole survivor of the attack on Matthew's Humvee.

Some people would undoubtedly consider Brian lucky, but we're not sure we would agree. He's doing as well as can be expected today. He suffered from survivor's guilt, like so many of the young men and women who come home from war. And at a very young age of nineteen he has been irrevocably changed by what he has seen and experienced on the battlefield.

Four men, four young heroes, lost their lives that day. We would argue that the true total was five. The life that Brian Daniels knew no longer exists. It ended on November 15, 2005, in a flash of fire and pain beside a dirt road on the other side of the world.

This Sucks — It Is What It Is

Stacey:

This sucks! In the early days of our grief journey, there were no plainer words than those. In our angriest, saddest moments, they became our phrase of the day. The words just seemed to fit the bill so perfectly, and they were far cleaner than cursing or using other words not worthy of repeating.

In an instant, our lives had been turned upside down — shaken — changed so radically that the phrase "this sucks" just seemed the easiest way to express my anger. To be honest, it still slips out on occasion, albeit far less often.

Every day that passes, I wish we could turn back the clock and have everything return to the way it was before that fateful day. What a blessing that would be to have Matthew working at the local coffee shop, perhaps going to college, or trying to figure out what he was going to do with his life. Instead, we've struggled to live our lives, and — somehow — to try to live Matthew's life as well. There are days when it makes me feel schizophrenic, but I don't know what else to do. I feel compelled to live this strange dual life, to keep my sanity. Our lives, and Matthew's, pals forever...

There have been days when I know John has asked God to mercifully take him out of this life, when he simply does not want to go on any longer. And then I watch him square his shoulders, pick up Matthew's flag, and start to move forward again; advancing, always advancing on the enemy. We've learned together that we can either lie in the dirt after being knocked down, or we can rise again, pick up a flag — a cause — and stumble forward.

There's an old saying, never kick a man when he's down. I say go ahead and kick him. If he's a man, he'll get up.

I don't have a problem with being kicked. It makes me stronger. What I don't like is people telling us to *'Get over it.'* We've realized over time that people only say such things because they don't know what else to say.

But there have been times, as John will tell you openly, when we've been tempted to smack the next person who utters those silly, thoughtless words... "You'll get over it."

Of course, we don't go around smacking people. Instead, we've done our best to gently correct them. The truth is that we'll *never* get over it. The loss doesn't go away. We've just become better at coping with it.

As odd as it might sound, I pray that we never get over it. That would mean I don't care about our son anymore, and that would simply be unthinkable.

You can't take a journey without baggage. I'm carrying our share of emotional baggage on my journey through grief. John often feels that somehow he is at fault, that he's to blame for what happened to Matthew. After all, he is the Dad, and dads are supposed to protect their families. He has never taken that task lightly. It was always foremost on his mind as Matthew was growing up.

John used to tell people that he was a pit-bull, and Matthew was his pup. He would have laid down his life in defense of our family.

It didn't come as any surprise to me that Matthew grew up to be so much like his father. Perhaps that's where some of John's guilt stems from. Matthew was a man's man, and he learned a lot of that from the example set by his father.

John always tried to lead by example. If he screwed up, John would apologize, and make sure that Matthew knew about it. That's what a man does. He admits his errors. He tries to correct them. He isn't afraid to own up to his mistakes.

There are times when John wonders aloud if he did a good enough job setting the example, or maybe even too good a job. Either one sounds a bit crazy, but sometimes we are a little crazy. That's part of this journey, too. There's plenty of room in the luggage rack for a few minutes of insanity, right next to the emotional baggage.

People have told John that Matthew's death was not his fault that he was a good father, and that's why Matthew turned out to be such a fine and brave man. John can accept the evidence logically. It helps when people remind him that it's not his fault.

I fervently pray that John will eventually release himself from the pain and struggle of his doubts. Maybe someday he will be able to lay down the burden of guilt that he carries. But that day has not come yet. Because, logical or not, the guilt feels to him every bit as real as the pain.

From the day Matthew was born, John was the ever-present, doting, sometimes over-protective parent. In Matthew's adolescent years, he often struggled with John's over-protectiveness. Perhaps he wished that his father would let go just a little. But the stories from Matthew's Army buddies confirm what we already knew. Matthew was his father's son till the very end.

If John was the rock of our home, I was the pillow, ever patient and adoring of our only child.

Matthew — our gift from God. Imagine that, God entrusting us with a child, a son to raise, leaving it to us to prepare this beautiful young boy to go out into the great abyss of the world.

Both of us took turns crying for the first several months after Matthew left home, back in 2004. Had we done everything right? Had we prepared him for all the potholes that life would throw into his path? Was he ready to withstand the ways of the world? Would he wander, making choices that we would have advised against? The answer to these questions and many more like them was simply, yes!

As parents, we sought God's help in providing us with a tool bag to work from. Our prayers began long before the day of Matthew's birth. We knew before our son ever took his first breath that we wanted to be good and loving parents. And we knew that we couldn't do it without the help of God.

It wasn't always easy being on the same page. Like most young parents, we sometimes disagreed. I would say yes to something, and John would say no. However, for the most part, we tried to not let Matthew see our disagreements. When we made decisions, he would usually see a unified approach from both of us. That unified front was important. It helped us to shape the man that Matthew became.

When Matthew was in our care, we frequently struggled with questions for which we had no good answers. That's not much of a surprise. Every parent deals with his or her share of unsolvable dilemmas. But even the death of our son has not stopped those questions from coming.

While time has brought some healing to the great hole in our hearts, the questions are still with us. Why? Why do bad things happen to good people? Why Matthew? Why this fine and caring young man, and not someone else who didn't give a darn about others? Why couldn't this happen to someone who did bad things, instead of a man who tried so hard to do the right thing?

We'll never know the answers to those questions, or any of the other "whys" that go along with them. After all, it is what it is. And somehow, by the grace of God, we have been able to put one step in front of the other.

So we keep stepping forward, keep carrying Matthew's flag, even when we can only manage a few inches at a time. And through it all, we've learned to put smiles on our faces. After all, who wants to hang around someone who's always down?

Because of Our Faith

John:

It's fair to say that it's not an easy road that Stacey and I now travel, but it's because of our faith in God that we have the strength to make the journey. I am so glad that I led Matthew to know Jesus Christ as his Lord and Savior at eight years of age. It gives Stacey and me peace and reassurance in the hope and knowledge that one day we'll be reunited with our son.

I often think about the last discussion Matthew and I had about his decision to enlist. Mind you, neither his mother nor I were against Matthew joining the military. It was understandable that he wanted to follow in the footsteps of family members before him.

We didn't try to prevent him from enlisting, but we made it clear that we preferred that he not choose a combat role. He was our only child, and Stacey and I both knew from our own military careers that the danger to his life was very real.

One of our last conversations prior to his swearing-in ceremony will forever be etched in my mind. I distinctly remember saying, "Matthew, if you join the Army you will probably go to Iraq, and you could be killed!"

Matthew looked at me and calmly replied, "Well Dad, you did a lot of dangerous things. You jumped out of helicopters. You were a police officer and a fireman, but nothing happened to you. Besides, I could step off a curb tomorrow, and get hit by a truck crossing the street. What would the difference be then?"

How could I respond to such profound and simple logic? *Yes I know son, but that was me, not you.* I could just imagine myself saying that to Matthew. And I could imagine his response.

Before I could say anything, Matthew spoke again. "Besides Dad, if something happens to me, I know where I'm going."

How do you argue with faith?

I will forever be grateful that I heard those words come from my son's mouth. They give me so much comfort each and every day, and they always will — until I am reunited with him in heaven.

Matthew was a warrior! I know that I should never have expected anything less from him. He was too much like his mother and me. We'd often say that he had a hard head and a soft heart, just like both of us.

When we received the news of his death, we were so devastated that pieces of us died along with Matthew. I have come to understand that, when that IED went off, we became part of the collateral damage.

I feel the old me was killed along with Matthew, on November 15, 2005, at 1715 hours Baghdad time. I went to bed that Wednesday evening, and the next day I was reborn into a new existence. The old John was dead. The new John — with all of his wounds — was struggling along on life support.

I had joined the ranks of the walking wounded. My ability to function was so greatly impaired that I was almost not the same person any more. Shock had set in. Post Traumatic Stress Disorder had gained a toehold within me and was growing like a poisonous weed. The only things I had to cling to were my faith, my family, my friends and most of all, my wife. In an instant, Stacey became the most important thing left to me on this earth. Of course, she was fatally wounded herself, but that didn't stop her from becoming my rock.

At times, she has clearly been far stronger than I. I realize that she was just as badly wounded, but she has been there every step of the way, helping me to limp along. In the months following Matthew's death, and through to this day, it has been her unswerving faith that has helped keep me alive. She has continued to believe in me far more than I have been able to believe in myself.

We both lost our appetites in those first weeks, and I think we lost some of our will to live at the same time. Neither of us slept well, and when sleep did come to us, it was fitful and restless. It came at the expense of many tears.

Between the two of us, we lost close to forty pounds in those first weeks. People became concerned about me, and they were worried about my mental state. In all honesty, they had good reason to be concerned. I felt like a hamster trapped in a motorized wheel going around, and around, and around... looking for a way out, and never finding it.

It was at that point I picked up the Bible and began to read the book of Job in the Old Testament. Like many Christians, I was loosely familiar with Job, but I had never bothered to sit down and read the complete story.

Frankly, before this tragedy struck our family, the lessons of Job had never felt particularly relevant to me.

Losing Matthew changed my viewpoint. Reading about Job and his struggles helped me to put my relationship with God into a proper perspective.

I could never bring myself to be mad at God. Somehow, even in my darkest moments, I knew better than to blame the Lord. I was confused then, and I'm still confused now. I think I'll probably remain confused until I pass on from this world, but in my heart I know being angry with God for my family's troubles will never solve anything.

Reading Job helped me realign my picture of our situation. Our family has been through a lot, but Job lost far more than Stacey and I ever will. And, all tears and doubts aside, Matthew is in a much better place than we are.

I'm only human. I am flawed. As strong as my faith is, it is not perfect. I must remind myself on a daily basis that it's true. Matthew really is in a better place. Those of us left here on earth must continue to go through the struggles of daily life. Matthew is beyond those struggles. He is safe in the arms of the Lord.

So, where does that leave me? What am I to do? While I'm left here on this earth, the answer is clear. My job is to be an example, to be willing to reach out and help others, until the day our Lord finally calls me home.

Stacey:

In our discussions over the past couple of years, John and I keep coming back to one important question. Did we teach Matthew enough about what to expect from the twists and turns of life? It's a question that every parent probably asks. In our case, we will never know the answer to that question this side of heaven.

Obviously, no one would wish the death of a child upon the shoulders of any parent. The loss of a child through military service brings its own set of challenges.

We are a Gold Star family. That's the term that describes an American family who loses one of its beloved members in combat.

Clearly, we did not ask to become a Gold Star family. We never had any desire to pay the tremendous price of admission to join this group. But we became members, despite our hopes and our intentions. We're here now. We're a Gold Star family. And now we're faced with new questions. How can we redirect our minds and emotions in such a way that we will honor the sacrifice that our son made? How do we honor Matthew's memory and the nation that he gave his life to defend?

During the course of Matthew's short life, we tried to teach him many lessons. There are two in particular that I want to share with others. I hope that doing so will provide some insight into why Matthew chose to be a Soldier, and how we can carry forward in his honor.

The first lesson is from Luke 12:48, *to whom much is given, much is expected*.

The second lesson, and perhaps the most powerful, is that life is full of reward and that one of the greatest rewards comes from taking your eyes off of yourself and putting them onto others. In other words, the Golden Rule.

In many ways, the second lesson has aided John and me in our journey of pain and grief. It has helped us to understand how our son applied these lessons. It reminds us that we can best honor him by continuing to apply those same lessons in our lives.

From the very beginning of Matthew's life, John and I worked to ensure that our son was given opportunities that many other children can only wish for. Don't misunderstand me. I'm not saying that we handed things to Matthew on a silver platter. We didn't. I'm also not suggesting that everything was perfect in our family. It wasn't. We had our differences, as most families do. My point is that Matthew had many choices available to him.

Some people join the military because they don't have any other good options. They may come from economically depressed areas, or military service may seem like the only path to a higher education. Whatever their backgrounds happen to be, some people enlist because they don't see any other choices.

That wasn't the case for Matthew. He had an entire world of opportunities. He was a skilled and gifted artist. His creative talents were visible from a very early age. He was also a gifted athlete, and a three-time U.S. National champion in Karate. He had a particular strength and patience when it came to working with children. And beyond all of that, he had us. John and I had worked hard to earn what we had and our family has been blessed with the success of our efforts.. We had the resources and the ability to help Matthew pursue any professional or educational path he wanted to follow.

Matthew *chose* to become a Soldier. He wasn't forced onto that path by lack of opportunity, but he chose the United States Army. He was well aware of the situation in Iraq, and he knew the risks he'd be facing by joining the Army in a time of war. He weighed the potential dangers against his sense of personal responsibility, and he made his decision with his eyes wide open.

As John has shared, we were proud of Matthew's decision to serve our nation, but we would have been much more comfortable if he had not chosen a role that would lead directly to combat. In the end, the choice was his to make.

Of course, we wanted to know *why* he would deliberately take such a risk. His answer was simple. He wanted to serve a cause much greater than himself.

Matthew was very conscious of how much he had been given, and he wanted to offer something in return. He wanted to share with others a taste of what it was like to have options. If he could share a little of the freedom that so many of us take for granted, if he could give others even a glimpse of hope for a better life, then he could apply the lessons we had worked so hard to teach him.

This became even clearer when Matthew selected his army specialty. He decided to become a Combat Medic, a job that called for him to face the perils of combat — not to *fight*, but to *heal*. He wanted to be the "Doc," to bring comfort and healing in the midst of war.

The last call we received from Matthew came just days before his death. It was one of those early morning calls, and he was very excited. He asked us to send him some color crayons. He had decided to teach the children in Iraq how to draw, to use his God-given talent to bring a bit of joy to a place that had known only fear.

When he hung up the phone at the end of that call, there was no way Matthew could have known that he had only a few days to live. There was no way for him to know how close the end was, or how rapidly it was approaching. But I'm not sure it would have made any difference if he had known. He had chosen his path, and I don't think he would have turned away from it. Even to his very last breath, he was working to bring light into darkness.

When John and I learned that our only child had been killed in a land half way around the world, we wanted our lives to end too. Since the moment of Matthew's birth, we had been a threesome, and now the little triangle that formed our family had been broken.

In the days and months following that terrible day, there were often times when John or I were ready for our lives to be over. We still feel it sometimes. But then we remind ourselves of how selfish such feelings are. Our work is not yet done here on earth. There are others who need our help.

To whom much is given, much is expected. It was true for Matthew, and it is no less true for us. We must be willing to take our eyes off of ourselves, and to put them onto others. Matthew's choices proved that he had learned to follow those lessons as well. If we truly want to honor our son, John and I can do no less.

Matthew was drawn to the children. John and Stacey received this picture on Matthew's digital camera following his funeral service. It was taken within a week of his death.

It hasn't been easy to pick up the shattered pieces. With our faith, and with help from others who are walking in our same footsteps, John and I are making every effort to refocus our lives. And, as we continue on this journey, I'd like to offer some of that peace and hope for those who are faced with pain and doubt, and don't know where to go.

Be willing to reach out to others. Be willing to touch another's life, to make a difference no matter how small it may seem. Refocus your eyes until you can see beyond your pain to others in need. In the end, the reward will be worth all the effort you have given.

The Walking Wounded

John:

Matthew was our bridge into the future, and as dearly as we love him, that bridge is now broken. Our family will not see another generation. We will never see our grandchildren. We will not see our bloodline, our values, and the culture of our family carried on into future generations. That dream is gone now. The loss of any child is bound to be devastating to their parents. However, the loss of a military service member during a time of war and in a combat zone puts a particularly harsh strain on families. This can be even truer when that son or daughter happens to be your only child.

Matthew represented the legacy of our family. In the aftermath of his death, we can only cherish the memories of his youth, and dream of what it would have been like to see our hero come home safely.

Some people call us the walking wounded. And sometimes, no matter how much strength we find in ourselves, in each other, and in our creator, that's exactly how we feel. *Wounded*!

Matthew's death tested our fortitude. It tested our faith. It tested our marriage. When the dust settled and Matthew had been laid to rest, Stacey and I found ourselves pulled in different directions. The house in San Diego held too many difficult memories for her.

Matthew had spent Christmas with us there in 2004, and it was the last place that Stacey had seen him alive. She returned to Idaho to be near her close and dear friend Louise, and to seek spiritual answers and a peace that she felt she wouldn't be able to find in San Diego. She needed time away from our California home, and the ever-present memories of Matthew.

I needed to stay in San Diego to be close to family and friends, and to be surrounded by the last house that Matthew had called home. Somehow it made me feel just a little closer to him.

Stacey's grief drove her away from our house in California. My own grief kept me away from our home in Idaho. For me, that's where the nightmare had begun. If I stayed in Idaho, I would find myself staring at the front door day after day, reliving those terrible moments when two strangers in military uniforms came to our door bearing the worst possible news.

So it was that Stacey and I spent much of that first year apart from each other. People face loss in different ways. There is not a right or wrong way to grieve. Each of us must find our own path. Stacey and I quickly came to understand that we both needed the space to begin healing.

We knew that we would come together again, but, for a while, we needed to be apart. Our lives have been shattered, and in those initial months we were trying desperately to pick up the pieces. We knew that we had to reassemble our slivers of hope into something resembling a life, but we had no real idea of how to go about it.

We were reunited in the late summer of 2006, when Stacey returned to San Diego. Our pain was still very fresh and very real, but we were together again, ready to face the next steps of our journey.

I cannot find the words to convey how deeply painful it is to lose your child. If you've been through such a loss, you already know what it feels like. If you haven't, I sincerely pray that you never have to find out.

The burden of my grief and my guilt were overwhelming. I began wracking my brain for some way to release the burden before it crushed me completely. Some of my ideas were probably just a little bit crazy, but quite frankly I didn't care. When your heart is hurting and truly broken, even the craziest ideas can begin to make sense to you.

That's how I ended up visiting the office of my local Army recruiter. Sure, I'm a middle-aged man, but I wasn't too old to be eligible for active duty. In fact, my prior service experience made me a good potential candidate for reenlistment. So, in April of 2006, I found myself sitting across the desk from a sharp-looking young Army sergeant.

The sergeant listened patiently as I told him about Matthew. He was respectful when I explained why I needed to go to Iraq, to face the danger that our son had faced, to try and finish the job that Matthew had started.

The sergeant regarded me solemnly, and assured me that he understood. But, did he *really* understand? Probably not. Almost certainly not. He hadn't lost his only child. How could he possibly understand?

He typed my information into his computer, consulted his recruiting database, and then immediately informed me that I needed to lose some weight.

I had already lost about twenty pounds in the weeks following Matthew's death and after leaving the recruiter's office, I embarked on a personal mission to get myself in shape for enlistment. With diet and exercise, I dropped another twenty pounds. Within six months of Matthew's funeral, I was down forty pounds.

Unfortunately, that was only the tip of the iceberg. Since my separation from the Army in June of 1981, I had gained nearly eighty pounds. Losing forty pounds only put me half way to my goal.

If my weight had been the only obstacle, I would have made the cut. I was driven. I was ready to make any sacrifice, and overcome any challenge. But I'm also diabetic, and I had other medical complications to go along with the diabetes.

Ultimately, my health didn't allow me to qualify for reinstatement to active duty, so although it may seem like my plan to reenlist was a waste of time, it wasn't. As crazy as it must have seemed to my friends and family, the experience was good for me. It gave me purpose. It gave me a goal. It forced me to turn my attention to the future instead of the past. And somehow, it stopped the suicidal thoughts I had been struggling with and gave me a reason to keep living.

At that moment in my life, I needed such a reason very badly. My buddy, my best friend aside from my wife, was gone. Life didn't mean much of anything to me. I was riding a roller coaster of wild emotions, and my days had faded into an indistinct blur of inactivity. My unsuccessful bid for reenlistment helped me to shift my focus, at least temporarily, away from despair.

Of course, my struggles were far from over. I began to play out scenarios in my mind, self-talk, if you will. I came up with an analogy that I shared with Stacey. It went something like this... The three of us — Matthew, Stacey, and I — had been in a train wreck, and Matthew had been killed. Stacey and I were still at the scene of the crash sitting in the dirt beside the wreckage. We were stuck there, day after day, just staring at this mangled mess of a train, and mourning Matthew.

I told Stacey that we had to get back on our feet and walk away from the wreck. If we didn't, we were going to wither away and die. Wounded as we were, we needed to start moving.

This was clearly something we would not be able to fix all by ourselves. We needed help...

Stacey:

Where do you go in time of crisis? Matthew's death brought that question to the forefront. Do you turn to family? Friends? Acquaintances? God? All of the above?

As I write these words several years later, it all seems like a blur. At the same time, it appears all too clear. Certainly our lives had been turned upside down.

John and I were in our mid-forties when this happened, in the prime of our lives, enjoying the fruits of our labor and living what many would consider a great life. That changed with absolutely no warning. The rug was pulled out from underneath us, and we could not find our way back to the life we had lost.

John and I were good people, and things like this were not supposed to happen to good people. What could we have possibly done to deserve this?

Our world had been shattered by the ringing of a doorbell. The echoes of that bell still resounded through our lives.

For the first many months and well into that second year, everything in our lives seemed to alternate between slow motion and a complete standstill.

There were those first phone calls, sharing the horrifying news with family and friends. Then came the nights of fitful sleep, and the nights when there was no sleep at all. John and I both began to lose weight. And through it all there were the tears, upon tears, upon tears. We were like broken faucets. Every time we thought we had finally cried ourselves out, we discovered yet another round of tears.

At first we tried to be discrete about it. A family's sorrow is a deeply private thing. After a while, we didn't care anymore. Our grief was laid bare to the world, to friends and strangers alike.

We were shrouded in memories ripped from the depths of our spirits. Our son was gone. Our legacy was lost. Our very hearts and souls had been taken from us. Gone. Finished. Never again would we feel Matthew's touch. No more hugs from our beautiful son. No more phone calls. Nothing. Gone! We cried, and to be honest we didn't really care who saw our tears.

Should I apologize if I sound a little bitter — perhaps just a tad angry? Why should I apologize?

Everyone has dreams. John and I certainly did. We had dreams for Matthew, dreams of his future marriage, a daughter-in-law, and — maybe someday — grandchildren to bless our lives even more. All of those dreams vanished in an instant.

It's been said that you can only learn the depth of true friendship when disaster hits your family. I sought solace in a few very close friends. They had no answers to the questions raised by Matthew's death. With the deepest respect, how could I really expect them to have answers?

What my friends *did* provide were heartfelt ears, and shoulders to lean on. They could not give me simple answers to my questions. Instead, we shared a common bond in our walk with Christ. My friends gave me comfort, strength, and support. Most importantly, they pointed me to the Lord for all the questions I had.

To be strong enough to walk through the darkness, to trust, and have the childlike faith that God could help John and me overcome the depths of our despair — this was our new journey. This is the path we've been given to walk. As difficult as it is to carry such a burden, our faith and belief in God has been the foundation of our strength. The Lord has given us the grace to carry this cross. It has brought us closer together as husband and wife, and allowed our hearts the time to heal.

I recall approaching the third anniversary of Matthew's death. The Thanksgiving holiday was just around the corner, and I found myself thinking about the sights and smells the holiday season brings. The aroma of pumpkin pie in the air mingled with the scent of turkey and ham, mashed potatoes, yams and all of the other fixings of a wonderful and blessed family affair.

It's a special time of year that encourages families to follow their own traditions. Some families bring out their beautiful tablecloths and lay the table with elegant settings. Other families serve potluck style on paper plates, with loved ones scrunched into every corner of the kitchen and dining room.

Wives and mothers are in the unique position of making the Thanksgiving holiday a special time for our families. Thanks to many special moments over the years, our family holds fond memories of Thanksgiving. It's always been one of our favorite times of the year.

That is, it *used* to be. In November 2005, everything changed. In the blink of an eye, all of our wonderful memories of Thanksgivings past were ripped away, and replaced by a sense of irredeemable loss.

In the weeks, months and even perhaps those first initial years following, I wasn't sure if we would ever regain the sense of joy and peace that Americans are supposed to feel in the season of thanks. Since that tragic day, I've used the approach of Thanksgiving to refocus my thoughts on what it really means to be truly thankful. As I've contemplated the deeper meaning of the season, I came across a few interesting facts that I felt were worthy of sharing.

We all know that the story of Thanksgiving stems from the days of the pilgrims. But when we think about the settlers at Plymouth Rock, we tend to concentrate on their sense of wonder and gratitude as they gave thanks for the blessings of abundance. We often forget the profound suffering they endured.

In the winter prior to that first Thanksgiving of 1621, nearly half of the pilgrims died. In fact, the first year in their new land was spent praying for their very survival. When they gathered to celebrate that first bountiful harvest in the new world, the memories of their loss must have still been fresh in their minds.

Nearly 150 years later, George Washington paused with his Soldiers under a cold November sky to give praise for the first Thanksgiving in the newly formed United States of America. Little did he know that a winter of bitter suffering awaited them in Valley Forge.

Almost 90 years after that, in 1863 after several years of Civil War, Abraham Lincoln asked all Americans to celebrate a season of Thanksgiving on the last Thursday of each November. For many of our ancestors, Thanksgiving was not only a celebration of all that was good. It was also a determination to honor God no matter the circumstances.

In most recent years, our leaders have been known to share that the first Thanksgiving was one of the many occasions on which our fellow countrymen paused to acknowledge their dependence on the mercy and grace of a gracious God.

As I considered these historical facts, I found myself relating to a much deeper meaning. Since Matthew's death, I've come to embrace the Thanksgiving season with a determination to acknowledge my dependence on the grace of our Lord, to offer Him all my thanks, in the happiest of times, and yes… even in the saddest of times. You see, without a thankful heart, I would find it much more difficult to reach out to others during this time of great blessing.

Without a doubt, our family has experienced times of abundant harvest for which we are most grateful, and Proverbs 15:15 tells us that *a cheerful heart is a continual feast*. Through the journey of these past several years, I believe that my once-cheerful heart has grown into a more thankful heart. What better gift can I give to those who have been such a positive influence to me in so many different ways? A glimpse of my gratitude is the most valuable treasure I can offer them.

Proverbs 15:13 shares that *a heartache crushes the spirit*. I've learned that I don't have to feel guilty, that I may not always have a cheerful heart at certain times of the year, and that's okay. I've learned to be more reliant on the Lord, and to have that spirit of thanks in all that I have been blessed with.

Just a short few years ago, I chose to stand on faith during a very difficult and heart-wrenching time for our family. I'll freely admit that during that time I often found it difficult not to succumb to my own emotions of despair and bitterness. But my strength is renewed when I remember to walk by faith, and not by sight.

As each moment of crisis has passed, I have returned to the foundation I've found peace in so many times before. I have been comforted as I read of the psalmist who poured out his complaints before the Lord in Psalms 142:2. This verse, among so many others, encouraged me to find a place with Him alone — a place where I could lay all of my challenges before the Lord.

Through many tears, I've shared with Him how unfair I think it was to take Matthew so soon. He was well loved. So many people enjoyed being with him. He should have had many more years before him. I've shared all these things with the Lord, and much more. And that simple act of laying my burdens at His altar has brought me a certain sense of release.

As I've taken steps to finally be willing to let Matthew truly go, it's become much easier to offer God my complete thanks. Along the way, I learned that an important part of finding my 'Attitude of Gratitude' comes from being completely honest and up-front with God. Only when I arrived at that point could I ask Him to help restore thankfulness to my heart.

When I arrived at that place of total surrender to His transforming power, it became so much easier to thank Him daily, no matter what life placed in my path.

In 1 Thessalonians, we are encouraged to "give thanks in all circumstances."

As a wounded soul, I found solace in Jeremiah 33:11 ...*give thanks to the Lord Almighty, for the Lord is good; his love endures forever*. I believe beyond a shadow of a doubt that no matter what I may come to face, I'll always be able to give thanks to the Lord for His goodness, and especially for His comfort and all-abiding love.

As the people of this country prepare for their Thanksgiving celebrations each year, my hope is that the Lord will give them a grace that goes far beyond potatoes, turkey, and pumpkin pie. I pray that each of them will be blessed with a thankful heart as they offer sincere thanks to our loving God. And I pray that they will follow the example of our pilgrim ancestors, and remember to lay a continual foundation of faithfulness for generations of families to build upon.

Hugs and Thumbs

John:

In June 2005, we received a call from Matthew informing us that he had been issued orders to deploy to Iraq with the 101st Airborne Division. As was typical with military orders to a combat region, the specific date and time were withheld for security purposes. Matthew had few details to share, other than to convey a rumor that his unit could possibly deploy in early October 2005 somewhere between three and four months following the initial notification.

There was no way I was going to let our son go to war without seeing him off. I immediately began making plans to fly out to visit Matthew before his unit left Ft. Campbell, Kentucky.

His mother and I hadn't seen him since he had come home to San Diego for Christmas leave in December 2004. All Christmas celebrations with Matthew were wonderful, but that one will forever be etched in our memories. In preparation for his arrival, I decorated the tree ahead of time. That was something Matthew traditionally did, so I left the angel off the top of the tree, figuring that he could finish the decoration himself.

As we had done in years past, we made a really big deal out of topping the tree. It probably took all of ten seconds, but we cheered and took pictures as Matthew placed the angel in its rightful place on the top of the tree. We shouted, "Yeaaahhh!" and "Welcome home, Son!" We had no way of knowing that it would be Matthew's last Christmas on earth.

After his call in June 2005, I made a special point to stay in close contact with him. I wanted to be sure I kept up on the latest information about when his unit would deploy.

August came, and everything pointed toward the 101st leaving Fort Campbell in late September or early October. They would fly to Kuwait first, and then into Iraq.

As the departure date drew closer, I finalized my arrangements to travel to Kentucky and spend time with Matthew prior to his deployment. Stacey and I had just relocated to the Pacific Northwest, and she was starting a new job, so we decided that I would make the trip alone.

John, Stacey and Matthew celebrating their last Christmas together December 2004. This would be the last time Stacey saw Matthew.

I made reservations to fly out on September 14, with a return flight on September 18. Matt's 21st birthday was on the 19th, and I was happy to know that I'd be able to wish him an early Happy Birthday in person.

Matthew and I spoke on the phone about a week before I was scheduled to leave, as I wanted to confirm my arrival time at Fort Campbell. My greatest hope was that he'd be able to carve out enough time to visit with me.

From our conversation I could sense that Matthew was under a lot of stress. He was understandably nervous about the impending deployment. At one point, he even suggested that it might be better if I didn't fly out to see him. The entire unit was going through many hours of intense last-minute preparation and training, and he was concerned that he would be too busy to spend any quality time with me.

I told him I was coming anyway because there was no way that he was going to war without me seeing him first. I never told Matthew, but I kept thinking that if something did happen to him I would have trouble living with myself knowing that I had missed the opportunity to go visit him. I wasn't willing to take that chance. I was going to see our son.

On September 14, 2005, I departed Spokane with mixed emotions. I was excited and eager to see Matt, but I was fearful of the thought that our son, our only child, was heading off to war. Regardless of my fears, I was determined to make the most of this trip. I was going to make our time together as fun and relaxing as I could manage.

As trips go this one was fairly uneventful. Due to the timing and options of flights I ended up flying into Atlanta, Georgia with the intent of driving over to Kentucky. As soon as I was on the ground I rented a car, loaded up my luggage and made the four-hour drive to Fort Campbell.

I hadn't stepped foot in Fort Campbell since the late 1970s, when I had served there as a Military Policeman assigned to the 553rd Military Police Company, attached to the 101st Airborne Division. A friend and I had signed up under the 'buddy' program, with a request that we both go to Air Assault School after completing our basic and military police training.

Shortly after my buddy and I arrived there in September 1978, I earned my Air Assault jump wings. That's an exciting moment in any Soldier's career, but I had discovered something even more exciting. While going through our initial Army training back in Fort McClellan, Alabama, I met a girl. Not just *any* girl... *The* girl.

Her name was Stacey Allen and she was a fellow Soldier. I didn't know at that point that she would turn out to be the love of my life. I certainly had no idea that she would be my future wife, but I did know that she was incredibly cute, and I couldn't stop thinking about her.

So I was more than a little heartbroken when Stacey completed her training at the Military Police school and was transferred to the 980th Military Police Company at Sierra Army Depot in Herlong, California. That was all the way on the other side of the country, and to me it seemed like she would be another world away.

Yet I learned in those early days of our relationship that distance means nothing to true love. If Stacey were in California, I would go there, too. I did a little fancy footwork, and managed to get myself transferred to Herlong in February, 1979. Stacey and I were together again, and in September of that year we were married.

These memories were rolling through my mind as I made the drive from Atlanta to Fort Campbell. I was going to meet my son in the very place that I, too, had trained as a Soldier.

I arrived at my hotel outside of Fort Campbell and after the usual rigmarole of checking in, I settled down to watch some TV while I waited for Matthew to arrive. I was antsy and just a little charged with nervous anticipation. This was the first of five days we would have together and the time seemed too precious to waste sitting around a hotel room.

Finally, I heard the knock I'd been waiting for. I swung the door open, and there he was. I gave him a big hug and two thumbs up, our usual greeting. Most can understand the hug, but the thumbs part takes a bit of explaining. It was a private thing, its meaning known only to our family.

A sign of love between father and son, just eight weeks before Matthew was killed. John flew to Ft. Campbell to celebrate Matthew's 21st birthday and say farewell.

When Matthew reached his early teens like most young men in his age group he got to the point where he wasn't much into hugging Mom and Dad, especially in public. So, I got an idea from a family TV show that Matthew and I watched regularly. On one of the episodes, the father ran up against the same situation with his teenage son. After years of cheerful hugging, the son developed a sudden aversion to all outwardly visible forms of affection. To bridge the gap, the father and son developed a code sentence that meant, "I love you." Whenever they were out in public, or whenever the boy's friends were around, they could exchange their private signal of love without causing the son any embarrassment.

After watching the show, I came up with "thumbs." It became our family's private code, a way for the three of us to share private messages of love. Matthew, Stacey and I could flash each other the thumbs at the mall, the movie theater or just about anywhere else. We could say, "I love you," in public, and no one outside of our family would be the wiser.

It was a simple yet powerful message for our family unit. For both Stacey and me it will forever remain one of the lasting memories of our times together.

I used to tease Matthew that when I passed away my tombstone was going to be a giant thumb. Of course, he would just roll his eyes at that. Never in a million years could I have guessed that it would end up being the other way around.

We kept up the thumbs tradition long after Matthew had grown out of his fear of public hugs. Any time Stacey or I ran into him, we would trade the thumb to say, "I love you."

That's one regret I believe Stacey and I will never have. We were never afraid to tell our son that we loved him. When he was still living at home it wasn't unusual for him to hear those words several times a day. We have no doubt that Matthew always knew that he was dearly loved.

So when Matthew arrived at my hotel room in Kentucky, it was natural for us to share hugs and thumbs. Afterwards, we sat around chatting for awhile before heading out to catch a bite to eat. I asked how he was feeling, and how his back was holding up.

Matthew had injured his back the year before during Air Assault School training. That's where the Army teaches helicopter operations, with the bulk of the training spent learning how to repel from a helicopter. As part of their training, Soldiers learn how to attach themselves to ropes and repel approximately 100 feet to the ground from an airborne helicopter.

Regardless of the exercises they went through during training, the most important thing to remember was to hook up to the rope properly. If the connection was not made correctly, a Soldier could leave the helicopter on a "suicide slide," unable to control their speed of descent and slam into the ground like a sack of cement.

Air Assault School also teaches path finding, rigging and sling loading. In recent years they've also begun to teach another technique called "fast roping," which wasn't around when I went through the school in 1978. That's how Matthew had injured his back, during a fast roping exercise.

We're not exactly sure how it happened and Matthew never shared all the details of his injury, but he did confide in me that he had hit the ground too hard, jolting something in his lower back. That's about all we ever found out about his training accident.

I remember when Matthew graduated. I couldn't help but look back to my own training all those years before. I know from personal experience how tough Air Assault School was, so I was very proud that he was able to graduate and earn his wings. He was a little banged up from the accident, but he was strong and proud.

I'll never forget the phone call we got after he earned his wings. I can still hear the excitement in his voice. "Now I can put my wings with yours, Dad."

That's exactly where his wings are today, in a box next to mine, together with twenty-one shell casings from the twenty-one-gun salute at Matt's memorial ceremony in Taji, Iraq.

Matthew and I talked about all kinds of things in my hotel room. He spent several minutes telling me about some Oakley gloves that he had bought to wear when he got to Iraq. He liked the gloves, because the knuckles were protected by Kevlar. As he pointed out, he could punch all kinds of things without hurting his hands.

His birthday was just around the corner, so I gave him a birthday card from his mom and me. Stacey had baked him three containers of pumpkin chocolate chip cookies — his favorite — for his birthday.

With these small gifts exchanged, Matthew and I headed out to dinner at a sandwich shop just off post. We both ordered roast beef, one of our shared favorites. Our conversation continued on mostly with small talk, and when the sandwiches were gone we decided to call it a night.

Matthew drove me back to the hotel. As he dropped me off in the parking lot, we exchanged thumbs, and off he went. Day One was over, no sooner than it had begun.

My recollection of the next two days is a little hazy. It never occurred to me that I'd be sharing my thoughts in a book someday. As it turned out, Matthew and I only had a couple of hours to spend together each day. Most of my time was spent at the hotel waiting for him to get off duty, so we could spend what I've learned to look back at as very precious time together.

The highlight of Day Two was Matthew showing me the Kevlar gloves he had talked about the evening before. He was so excited about those gloves, just like a kid with a Christmas present.

Every time I imagine that scene, I smile. Matthew handed his new gloves to me, so I could check them out. Of course, being Dad, I had to look inside the cuffs to see if he had written his name in there. He hadn't.

Still stuck in Dad mode, I suggested that he write his name inside the gloves to keep people with sticky fingers from helping themselves. The gloves were pretty cool, and they seemed to be worth every bit of the $80 he had paid for them. If they protected his hands properly, it would be money well spent.

Before we called it a night, I told Matthew to bring a few friends along with him the following evening, and I would buy dinner for them. He reminded me that everyone in his unit was dealing with crazy last-minute schedules. He'd have to see if any of his buddies could join us. We gave each other hugs and thumbs again, and said goodnight.

The next evening was Friday, and Matthew brought Shawn Farrow along, a fellow Soldier who'd gone through training with him at Air Assault School. Like Matt, Shawn was also a combat medic, and sometime during the course of their training they'd befriended each other and learned that they were both from San Diego. In fact, it turned out that they had grown up within five miles of each other. It was obvious from the first time I saw them together that they had become very close friends.

As the three of us walked out to the parking lot, we stopped and I took a few pictures of Matthew and Shawn together. I then handed the camera to Shawn and he snapped a few pictures of Matthew and me, and then we headed out to dinner.

After ordering our meals and waiting for them to arrive, I remembered to ask Matthew about the cookies that Stacey had baked for him. He confessed that both Shawn and he had gobbled them up that first night I gave them to him. Looking back, I'm glad he enjoyed those cookies so much, and I'm glad that he was able to share them with a close friend.

Stacey hadn't seen Matthew since Christmas, nine months earlier, and she wasn't at all happy that her new job had kept her from making the trip with me. Those cookies traveled thousands of miles, and passed from my hands to Matthew's and with them a very simple message of love — from mother to son. I know that he understood the language of that message perfectly, that's why he chose to share those treasured cookies and his birthday gift with his closest Army buddy.

The weekend finally arrived, and we were able to spend most of Saturday together. Matthew picked me up in his black Ford F-150, and we drove over to Fort Campbell to the base PX, short for Post Exchange, a shopping mall for military personnel. I vaguely remembered the Fort Campbell PX from twenty-six years earlier. The PX we visited was much different than the one from my days on post. Matthew showed me around and pointed out various sites. From what I can recall we didn't buy anything that day. To be honest I was just enjoying spending time with my son.

Spending time with my son... Those words reminded me of the day Matthew was born at our home in Post Falls, Idaho back in 1984.

Memories came flooding back to that very special day, one I could remember perfectly as if it was just yesterday. The instant I caught sight of that beautiful little miracle, I shouted, "It's a boy!" He was exactly what I had hoped and prayed for.

Matthew and I left the PX, and walked next door to a small uniform store. I bought some souvenirs for myself as a reminder of my trip.

We stopped for a quick bite of lunch, and then we went to find a holder for Matthew's water pouch so he could attach it to the back of his Kevlar vest. The shop he was looking for turned out to be quite a drive, but we eventually located it. We found the gear he wanted, and made our way back to town. Somehow all of those little errands had used up nearly the entire day. We stopped for dinner, and then headed back to the hotel. After exchanging hugs and thumbs, we said our good nights.

The next day, Sunday, would be our last day together, and Matthew told me before heading back to the barracks that night that he would only be available for a couple of hours. The 101st was deploying to Iraq in two weeks, and Matthew's unit was going into overdrive with last-minute preparations. The next morning we worked out the details of our final rendezvous on the phone. Matthew and Shawn would meet me at a local steak house for dinner.

Everyone was all smiles when we got together. The three of us laughed and jibber-jabbered just like we had a few nights earlier, but as the evening wore on there was an obvious heaviness in the air.

I wanted these last hours to be perfect for me and for Matthew. But there was a tiny shadow in my heart. From the moment I had decided to make this trip, a single thought kept coming back to my mind. This might be the last time I would ever see my son.

I'll be honest. I was very concerned that our only child was heading off to war. Despite the newspaper stories, I knew that most of the Soldiers who deployed to Iraq came back in one piece. So I knew that the chance of something happening to Matthew was very slim, but it was a chance still the same.

Of course, there wasn't much I could do about it anyway. Matthew was his own man. He had made the honorable decision to serve in our country's military during a time of war. Everything was out of my control, completely and totally out of my hands.

Matthew, Shawn and I managed to make it through dinner. And then the moment came to say goodbye. We headed out to the parking lot and snapped a few final pictures. When the cameras had been put away, it was time for one last final hug. I started to cry. Looking at Matthew, I said to him, "I wish I could go with you."

My boy was headed off to war, and there was nothing I could do about that. There was no way for me to intercede, or to protect him. He was going into danger, into harm's way. I felt this need to be there to watch over him as I had always done, but now it was up to the grace of God to protect my son and all of those who were deploying with him.

The tears began to flow even harder. As we hugged, Matthew patted me on the back and said softly, "Dad, don't worry. I'm not going to die."

Every time I think about that moment, that final hug, I get choked up. That was the last hug I would ever receive from my son on this earth, the *very* last hug. Until the day I take my own final breath, I will never forget that moment. It's forever etched in my memory.

If you have never experienced such a traumatic loss, it's probably difficult for you to imagine what that kind of grief feels like. To someone who hasn't been there, the depth and persistence of the pain defies all logic. But trust me — *it's real*. And it doesn't go away! Even the simple act of writing these words brought tears to my eyes. I can't think about the last few moments that Matthew and I had together without getting choked up.

Somehow, I finally let go of him. I looked at those beautiful blue eyes of his, and gave him what would turn out to be our very last thumbs. "I love you!" I said. "Be safe. Keep your head down, and don't do anything stupid." Then we parted, and the three of us walked to our vehicles.

I drove out of the parking lot, and moments later I was on the highway headed back to my hotel. I was still thinking about that last hug and those last words, when the blare of a car horn grabbed my attention. I looked over to my right, and there was Matthew driving beside me in the next lane, smiling and waving. I waved back, and Matthew accelerated away with Shawn following close behind him.

I sped up trying to keep their vehicles in sight. I was pretty close to catching them when I had to slow down for the entrance to my hotel. Regretfully I had to step on the brake pedal, keeping my eye on Matthew's truck until it disappeared into the distance. I had no idea that this would be the last time I saw my son alive.

Stacey:

"*Regrets, I've had a few. But then again, too few to mention...*" The words of that old Frank Sinatra song played over and over in my mind in those early days after receiving the news of Matthew's death.

By my very nature, I'm not one who typically looks back with regret. I don't usually dwell on the *would*-have, *could*-have, and *should*-have scenarios in life. My regrets have been few, just as the song implies. But in those first months — and even the first year or two after Matthew's death — I regretted not asking for a few days off to get on that plane with John. I should have been there. Why had I missed that last opportunity to see our son alive?

Pragmatic by my very nature, I simply refused to think that anything would happen to Matthew when he went overseas. After all, we had lost so few of our men and women up to that point. By October 2005, several hundred thousand troops had been deployed to Iraq, and just over two thousand had lost their lives in combat related situations.

From the standpoint of probability, Matthew had more chance of dying in a car accident back in the states than he did serving a tour of duty in Iraq. In fact, shortly after we received word that Matt's unit was deploying to Iraq, John had placed a call to Matthew's captain. He assured John that he had taken approximately ninety men to Iraq at the beginning of the war, and he had brought the same number home alive, without a scratch. There we had it. The odds were greatly in favor of Matthew coming home safely.

In part it was that knowledge that contributed to my decision not to accompany John on the trip to Fort Campbell. Instead, I decided to send Matthew a message of love in the form of something I knew he would appreciate — his favorite cookies.

When I think about it, cherished memories of our family holidays come flooding back to me. When Matthew was growing up, I always baked pumpkin chocolate chip cookies during the Thanksgiving and Christmas. It was a special treat that I saved just for the holiday season.

Knowing that Matthew wouldn't be home for the holidays that year, I thought he would appreciate the gesture, and in particular the significance of the twenty-one cookies for his upcoming twenty-first birthday. Given that the cookies were all munched in a single evening, I can only assume that he enjoyed the gift.

I obviously can't go back. That moment in time has passed, and the opportunity of seeing Matthew just prior to his deployment is forever lost. Except for baking those cookies and missing my son, I have no memories of that period to look back on. The memories I now hold on to are of that last holiday season in 2004, when Matthew was able to come home for Christmas.

Because of our faith, I cling to the knowledge that one day John and I will be reunited with our son in another life — a life that will surely offer our world an indescribable peace. Until then, I cling to our faith and reach out to others who are following the same journey that John and I are on.

After all, they are the ones who can most relate and truly understand the pain we each endure.

Welcome Home, Son

John:

Sunday morning, November 20, 2005 was cold and foggy. We arrived at Spokane International Airport at 5 a.m. for our flight to San Diego. Within twenty-four hours of being notified of Matthew's death, Stacey and I had decided that he would be laid to rest in San Diego. After all, he had spent most of his growing years there, and it seemed like the right thing to do for the rest of our family.

We were both still emotionally shell-shocked as we settled in for the flight down south — hiding our tears behind sunglasses, speaking in muted voices, trying to avoid conversations with the other passengers on our plane.

After a short flight to Seattle and a transfer of planes, we were back in the air for the second leg of our journey. Two and a half hours after we left Seattle we touched down in San Diego.

We had been told by our Casualty Assistance Officer (CAO) in Idaho that another CAO, an Army Master Sergeant (MSG), would be standing by to meet us when we landed, and that's exactly what happened. MSG Paul Klickas was waiting for us as we exited the security area at San Diego's Lindbergh Field.

He was tall, maybe six foot four, and he appeared to be in his mid-to-late thirties. He looked so sharp in his dress greens that he could have posed for an Army recruiting poster. After the obligatory exchange of handshakes, he informed us that he had been assigned to handle our military liaison affairs while we were in San Diego.

We spoke with MSG Klickas for a few more minutes, and confirmed that we were scheduled to meet with a funeral director and his assistant the following morning, to begin making arrangements for Matthew's services. The Master Sergeant confirmed his knowledge of our meeting, and walked us through what he understood the process to be. He also gave us his contact phone numbers and told us if we needed his assistance in any way during the meeting to contact him immediately.

We kept our appointment the next morning and at first everything went as MSG Klickas had predicted. Then we got our first surprise. The funeral director informed us that he had received word from the Army that Matthew would be arriving in San Diego later that same day. This news caught both of us off guard, because prior to leaving Idaho, we had been informed that — due to the Thanksgiving holiday — it would take approximately a week to receive DNA confirmation, and prepare Matthew for out-processing through Dover Air Force base. Now, we were being told that Matthew would be arriving home at around 8:30 that evening.

The funeral director asked if we wanted to be at the airport when Matthew's plane arrived. This struck us as a rather odd question. *Of course* we wanted to be there for the arrival of our son.

I asked the funeral director to explain the process of Matt's arrival. What steps were involved? What would the sequence of events be?

He began by telling us that Matthew would be flown into San Diego's Lindbergh Field, by commercial airline. Stacey and I exchanged glances. This little bit of news immediately raised a red flag in both of our minds, but we decided to let it pass for the moment without comment.

The funeral director then went on to inform us that Matthew's casket would be stowed in the cargo hold of the aircraft, with a military escort riding in the passenger cabin, carrying the flag that would drape the casket at Matthew's funeral.

I nodded slowly. "Okay."

The funeral director went on to describe the protocol that the airline could be expected to follow after the plane arrived at the terminal. First the passengers would disembark, and then their baggage would be off-loaded from the cargo hold. Finally, the baggage handlers would use a forklift to load Matthew's casket onto a luggage cart, and haul him as cargo over to the freight terminal, where the casket would sit amongst crates of car parts and tennis shoes until we arrived to claim it.

By this point, we were both overcome with anger and confusion. Stacey and I are both veterans, and we've descended from a long line of military veterans on both sides of our family. Our family understood the meaning of service and sacrifice. Now, we were being told that our son — a fallen American hero — was going to be welcomed back to the soil of his hometown with no more respect than a pallet of pipe fittings. Needless to say, this was not what we had envisioned.

I interrupted the funeral director's explanation, and informed him that was not how our son, who made the ultimate sacrifice for God, family, and country, was going to return home.

I excused myself, and stepped into the hallway to call our Casualty Assistance Officer. When MSG Klickas answered the phone, I repeated to him the explanation that Stacey and I had just received. I told him flatly that this could not stand. This was not how our son was going to come home. It wouldn't be acceptable for a returning General, or the President of the United States, and it was not acceptable for Specialist Matthew John Holley.

As we discussed the issue, I could hear the emotion in MSG Klickas' voice. He agreed that the procedure I was describing was not right, and he assured me that he would do everything in his power to ensure that Matthew received a proper reception upon his arrival into San Diego.

He asked for clarification on our wishes, and I described what we had in mind. Stacey and I were to be allowed onto the tarmac, to welcome our son home. Matthew was to be rendered full honors by a U.S. military honor guard, and then the honor guard would transfer his casket to a waiting hearse. After Matthew was transported to the funeral home, the honor guard would transfer him into the funeral home, again rendering appropriate honors.

In our minds, these were the honors befitting Matthew's sacrifice. We didn't think they were unreasonable then, and now, with the benefit of hindsight, we still don't think they were unreasonable. In fact, we have trouble imagining any suggestion that our fallen warriors deserved anything less.

After sharing our thoughts and concerns with Paul Klickas, I returned to the meeting room and informed Stacey and the funeral director that our CAO was working to resolve any misunderstandings.

It's fair to say, having never been through anything like this before in our lives, Stacey and I were completely stressed out. Even without our misgivings about the idea of receiving our son as a piece of freight, the very last thing we wanted to do was discuss all the different options available for burying our child, and we certainly didn't want to discuss how much it would cost to do so.

Absolutely nothing had prepared us for these circumstances. At various intervals throughout the discussion, the director or his assistant would turn to us and apologize. One or the other of them would remind us that everything was going to be okay, and that somehow — with God's grace and mercy — we would get through it.

As we proceeded with the preparations, the funeral director stepped out to take a phone call. When he returned, he said he had good news. MSG Klickas had called and informed him that he had received confirmation from the commanding rear detachment at Fort Campbell, Kentucky, home of the 101st Airborne Division. Matthew had deployed to Iraq with the 101st, and they would be expediting an honor guard to San Diego. They were scheduled to be on the ground in time for Matthew's arrival, but there was a new problem. The airline contracted to transport Matt's remains was not being cooperative.

As we were to learn later, the airline representatives felt that they were too busy conducting their normal business to allow any delay for the rendering of honors. Additionally, due to heightened security regulations they were not willing to allow Stacey and me on the tarmac to greet our son's remains, and they certainly didn't intend to allow the honor guard onto the tarmac either. The airline representatives felt that their plan to haul Matthew's casket to the freight area was quite adequate. Needless to say, we didn't agree.

The matter still hadn't been resolved when we wrapped up our other arrangements and left the funeral home about an hour or so later. The clock was ticking, and Matt's arrival in San Diego was drawing closer by the minute, but we still didn't know what that arrival was going to look like. Would he be welcomed home with honors? Or would he be hauled by a forklift into a cargo warehouse?

By the time we headed home, we were both completely exhausted. We would return to the funeral home later that evening, for the ride to the airport. The issue with the airline was still unresolved.

MSG Klickas remained in contact with us throughout the day, but by early evening we still didn't know if Stacey and I would be allowed on the tarmac at Lindbergh Field.

At around 5:30 p.m., our phone rang and Stacey answered the call. After a brief conversation with the gentleman on the other end of the line, she handed the phone to me. The caller was from Senator Barbara Boxer's office, one of our California representatives. At literally the eleventh hour, MSG Klickas had been able to connect with Senator Boxer's office, and they had agreed to assist in facilitating a resolution for our concerns.

The caller asked me to explain our desires for welcoming Matthew home, and I found myself repeating all of the things I had said to MSG Klickas earlier that day. I explained our desire to be on the tarmac when Matthew's remains were removed from the plane, and our intent to have a full honor guard render the appropriate military courtesies. "No offense," I said, "but forklifts and baggage handlers are simply not part of the program."

The caller listened patiently, and in an obvious attempt to seek some point of compromise, asked me if we would settle for anything less.

Without hesitation, I assured him that we would not accept anything less than the honors befitting our fallen Soldier.

He told me that he would make some phone calls, and see what he could do. I suggested that he might want to consider placing his first call to the Federal Aviation Administration (FAA) at Lindbergh Field; after all they controlled everything that happened with inbound and outbound air traffic. He thanked me for the suggestion, and we ended the call.

By this time, there were only two and a half hours before Matthew was scheduled to arrive in San Diego. If anything was going to happen, it would have to be very soon. We were running out of time.

About thirty minutes later, our phone rang again. It was Senator Boxer's representative calling back to inform us that everything had been cleared, and our requests were being granted.

It was the first piece of good news to come our way since the notification of Matthew's passing had reached us just five days earlier. As I hung up the phone, I thanked the representative profusely. Within minutes, we were on our way to the funeral home for Matthew's homecoming.

When we arrived at the funeral home, we still had a few minutes to wait before the ride to the airport. We had been joined earlier in the evening by our very close friends, Stephen and Rebecca Meyer, who were like a second set of Godparents to Matthew. We were awaiting the arrival of Wayne Pratt, my closest friend of forty plus years — affectionately known to Matthew as Uncle Wayne.

Minutes later, Wayne appeared outside at the corner of the funeral home building. Immediately I could see the tears welling up in his eyes. He walked over, and we hugged. The tears flowed freely between two grown men, and our mutual loss made us completely unashamed.

Wayne was more than Matthew's honorary uncle. He was as close to me as any of my brothers, far more than just my best friend. The three of us shared a common bond. We were Soldiers. Like Matthew and me, Wayne had served with the 101st Airborne Division, home to the Screaming Eagles. He was a member of our band of brothers. He was our Brother in Arms.

Wayne and I joined the others in the funeral home's limousine for the ride to the airport. In terms of distance, it wasn't a very long ride. It couldn't have been more than a few miles, but every second seemed to carry the weight of weeks, even years. It was the longest journey of my life.

The car was filled with people, but it was unnaturally quiet. The pounding in my head and my heart were a thousand times louder than any words that were spoken. Stacey and I were both locked in silent struggles to control our emotions, and neither of us was doing a very good job.

We finally arrived at the airport, and the driver was directed to the security gate outside the tarmac. Shortly after parking, we were met by the area Director of Homeland Security who introduced himself as retired Marine Corps Brigadier General Michael Aguilar. He was joined by the head of the San Diego division of the Transportation Security Administration, who himself was a former Air Force Captain, and accompanying them was the head of the San Diego Harbor Police for Lindbergh Field. All three gentlemen offered us their sincere condolences, and explained that everything was being prepared for our drive out to the aircraft.

Sometimes God places individuals in our paths for a purpose, and that evening, we were witnessing his handiwork in action. Those three gentlemen, and the personnel who assisted them, were superb in every way. They were extremely respectful and exceptionally reverent. They clearly understood the gravity of the situation and the mission with which they had been entrusted.

After a delay of only a few minutes, our driver was given clearance to drive out onto the tarmac, escorted by the San Diego Harbor Police. The Director of Homeland Security rode in the limousine with us for the short drive out to meet Matthew's plane.

We drove through the gates and slowly progressed onto the tarmac, making a sweeping left hand turn and heading west toward the waiting aircraft. My anxiety level was off the scale.

The driver followed the escort of Harbor Police vehicles with their lights flashing. Slowly, we continued winding our way through the dim lights and around several parked aircraft. We made another left turn, passing the tail of another plane.

That's when we caught the first site of Matthew's flag-draped casket.

I was overcome by a roiling chaos of conflicting emotions of grief, and I'm certain that Stacey was too. At the same time, I was proud of Matthew, proud of his strength, and his courage, and his heroism. And despite the heartbreaking circumstances of his return I was glad that our hero, our son whom I had hugged and said goodbye to just eight weeks earlier, had come home into the arms of his family.

Stacey and I exited the limo, and stood with our friends on the runway. I couldn't hold back any longer. I cried profusely while holding Stacey to my side.

Matthew's casket lay at the bottom of the aircraft's luggage ramp. The hearse was parked to the left, flanked by MSG Klickas with the honor guard from Fort Campbell positioned at full attention. To their right stood a small contingent of Harbor Police, also at full attention.

With everyone in their appointed place, the ceremonies began. The salutes were exchanged, and full honors were rendered. Stacey and I were completely focused on Matthew, and the military rites being performed in his honor. Neither of us noticed the crowd of spectators who had stopped to watch these solemn rituals.

We learned about the onlookers later, when Stephen Meyer shared his own observations with us. A mass of people had been pressed against the glass enclosure inside the terminal. Some of them had probably just disembarked from Matthew's plane, and others were undoubtedly awaiting the next flight out. Perhaps some of them were fully aware that they were witnessing the return of a fallen American hero, or perhaps not. I can't imagine what they might have been thinking.

Based on the initial resistance we faced in arranging those simple honors, it seemed possible — perhaps even likely — that no San Diego airline passenger had ever witnessed such an event on the tarmac at Lindbergh Field.

We were never able to properly thank everyone involved in pulling together the preparations in the hours before Matthew's arrival. Based on the information we'd been given, we had expected to have a week or so to arrange proper honors for our son's return. Instead, it all had to be done at the last minute, and Stacey and I will be forever grateful to all of the people who worked so hard and so quickly to honor our wishes and to see that our fallen hero — an American son — receive the honor he was due.

The honor guard transferred Matthew's casket to the hearse, and we reentered the limousine for the ride back to the funeral home.

When we arrived, Stacey and I approached the hearse. The funeral home attendants had opened the back door and were preparing to remove Matthew when I stopped them. I explained that it was our request to have Matthew's casket handled only by military personnel.

At first the funeral home attendants hesitated, but they quickly realized that I was steadfast in my determination. They stepped back to await the arrival of the military honor guard.

Stacey and I approached the casket and laid our hands on Matthew for the first time. Once again I began to cry, harder than I ever had before. I reached down to hug the casket. It was the closest I could come to hugging my son at that moment.

I talked to Matthew through my tears, and I stayed with him until the honor guard arrived. I only backed away as their formation marched slowly toward the rear of the hearse, and they ceremoniously carried Matthew's casket into the funeral home.

Inside, they lowered the casket onto its pedestal, and rendered the final honors and salutes.

At that moment, the escort who had flown with Matthew from Dover Air Force Base stepped forward, and presented us with a small black velvet bag. He quietly informed us that he was assigned to the rear detachment personnel unit at Fort Campbell and that he had known Matthew prior to his deployment to Iraq.

I slowly opened the bag. It contained Mathew's dog tags and his digital watch. I stared at the watch. It was running perfectly, still set for the time in Iraq. There wasn't a scratch on it.

The irony was almost too great to bear. Our son had been killed by a massive explosion, but his watch had come home undamaged.

Pinned to the watchband was a small set of jump wings that Matthew had earned back in October 2004, from Air Assault School, the same school both his Uncle Wayne and I had attended in 1978.

As I continued to gaze at the watch in disbelief, the rest of the honor guard stepped forward to shake our hands, give hugs and offer their condolences. The tears were clearly visible in their eyes. This was a fellow Soldier, a battle buddy, and one of their own from the 101st Airborne Division.

Matthew's unit was called Task Force Baghdad — Band of Brothers. And under the banner of the Screaming Eagles, Matthew had met his rendezvous with destiny.

He had returned to the arms of his family, his friends, and the men and women of his unit. And we knew that in heaven, he was soaring amongst God's eagles.

Welcome home, Son!

An Honor Due

Stacey:

I... do solemnly swear that I will support and defend the Constitution of the United States against all enemies, foreign and domestic; that I will bear true faith and allegiance to the same... So help me God.

These words are spoken by every person who makes the decision to serve our nation. The precise wording of the oath may vary slightly depending on the individual's appointed role, be it an enlisted member of the armed services, an officer in the same, an elected official or even the President of the United States. In each case, the appointee or service member is asked to raise his or her right hand, prior to repeating the oath. And when the final words have been spoken, that person is bound to honor the commitment, even if the price is life itself.

It was with this understanding of commonality and shared sacrifice that John and I arrived back in San Diego to prepare for the arrival of our son, a fallen American hero. Our hearts were torn with grief and our minds were still utterly stunned, but somewhere beneath the terrible unreality of our loss we held the full expectation that Matthew would arrive home to a hero's welcome. What reasonable person could have expected anything less? Matthew had died fulfilling his oath to our nation. *Of course* that sacrifice would be treated with the fullest honor it deserved.

Needless to say, we were in for another shock. It didn't take us very long at all to realize that our understanding of a hero's welcome had virtually no resemblance to what the military had in mind.

We had a series of tense and often terse discussions with our Casualty Assistance Officer and other government personnel. As a result, we were able to ensure that Matthew's remains were welcomed home in a manner that honored his sacrifice and respected our expectations.

Yet even as John and I prepared for Matthew's Celebration of Life service and the military funeral that followed, we kept running into the same question. Why was the process set up this way? How could anyone believe that it was acceptable to treat the remains of our fallen warriors like common cargo?

I suppose you could argue that any bureaucracy, including the military, has a tendency to remove the human factor from its internal processes. That could be true, but there's such a thing as carrying a point too far. We were not the first grieving family to encounter this unfeeling mechanical process, or the lack of respect that it conveyed. But we had to ask ourselves what person, agency or committee decided to approve a protocol that treated deceased American service members in this callous manner?

Matthew decided to serve in the military because he wanted to make a difference in the world. As he told us before he enlisted, he wanted to serve a cause greater than himself. He had approached his service with that selfless attitude, and — when the time came to give the last full measure of devotion — he did so with eyes wide open.

John and I believe that such sacrifice should be honored. The Army could not restore our beloved son to life, but at the very least it could treat his remains with the dignity and respect due him. It could afford him the honors he had earned.

I still recall the surreal feeling that came over me on that Monday as we sat at the funeral home going over the preparations for Matt's return. As we learned what the military had in mind, I wanted to jump out of my chair and scream, *what do you mean we can pick our son up at the freight terminal?*

At first, I couldn't believe that I had heard correctly. Surely that wasn't right. Surely they were not telling me that Matthew's casket would be carried by forklift to the oversized freight area where we could claim it from among the crates of roofing shingles and big screen televisions.

But as crazy as it sounded, that was precisely what the military had planned. This was the manner in which our nation's fallen heroes were being welcomed home.

It was callous and insensitive, and in my opinion completely disrespectful. But above all else, it was wrong. Matthew deserved better than that. So did every man and woman who made the ultimate sacrifice in the defense of this country.

Someone had to speak up. *Someone* needed to change things. And John and I quickly realized that *we* would have to become that someone.

But there would be time for that later. We could take on the challenge after we'd had an opportunity to properly grieve for our son. We could do it after we went to Atlanta to pick up Matthew's personal belongings. We could do it *after…*

After *what*? What were we waiting for? We've all heard the old saying, "there's no time like the present." If we were going to tackle this challenge at all, we might as well get started.

We had to move mountains in order to welcome our son home on the tarmac at Lindbergh Field on that cool November evening in 2005. We had a lot of help, for we alone could not have possibly managed such an enormous task. The expediting of the honor guard from Matthew's unit in Fort Campbell, the grounding of an American airliner, the closure of the airspace surrounding Lindbergh Field. Many coordinated events needed to unfold before John and I — along with a few of our closest friends — could enter the secured area of the airport to welcome our only child home to American soil. To this day we're still amazed at the support we received, and more so how quickly those mountains moved. Otherwise, we would never have been ready in time for Mathew's arrival back to San Diego.

Since Matthew returned home the week of Thanksgiving, John and I made plans for his services to be held the week after the holiday, to allow family and friends to travel to San Diego. After concluding the preparations for the Celebration of Life and the military honors services, we spent the remainder of our week slogging through government paperwork, arranging ceremonial events and coordinating visits with family for the pending holiday dinner.

John and Stephen Meyer continued to work on a project that they had started prior to leaving Idaho. They were putting together a video for the Celebration of Life service that we had planned for the evening before the military honors service. It was our desire to honor the young man who had touched so many lives in his short time here on earth.

There were meetings with our pastor, discussions on music, and a lot of other arrangements to make. We even decided to hang a Welcome Home sign in front of the church the evening of the service. After all, regardless of the circumstances, Matthew was coming home into the arms of his loved ones.

Finally we assisted with flight arrangements and hotel accommodations for those who would be arriving the following week. Looking back, it all seems like a blur. I have no idea how we managed to handle all of the necessary arrangements with no clear memory of what we were even doing.

We were incredibly busy, but we didn't lose sight of our plan. We didn't forget that we had agreed to do our best to change the military's process for repatriating the remains of fallen service members with their loved ones.

*   *   *

Just a few days after Matthew's services, John and I started talking about the idea again. We should speak up, he said. Speak up for all of the fallen heroes who unfortunately would follow after Matthew. Speak up for those loved ones who might not have the knowledge or the courage to do what we had done for our son.

And so with our own hearts still heavy with sorrow, we set out to challenge a policy that dated back at least to the pre-Vietnam era. Policy or no policy, we were going to change the way that fallen American heroes were returned home to their loved ones.

It was time to follow the advice we had given so often to our beloved son, to take our eyes off of ourselves and put them on to others. And there were so many others, too many, who needed the change we were trying to bring about.

But where could we start? Who could we turn to? How could we begin the process of transforming a national policy?

Ultimately, the change we were looking for would require legislation at the federal level. A change of this magnitude would have to be argued on the floor of the Congress and Senate, but even that was not the end of it. The bill would require the signature of the President of the United States.

So it was on Friday, December 9, 2005, just seven days after laying Matthew to rest, that John and I sat down with news reporter Salvador Rivera and his cameraman, Mike Gleeson. The local ABC news affiliate KGTV 10 in San Diego wanted to hear our concerns. We saw it as the first step to raising public awareness of the issue.

The story hit the airwaves that evening as a headliner on the five o'clock news.

Television viewers all over the San Diego area were suddenly made aware of the controversy over how the military was transporting the remains of service members killed overseas. John and I had expected that part, but we weren't expecting the lead-in to the story, which included discussions and questions as to the impetus behind our cause.

The story didn't end with the broadcast, and neither did the questions. After the story aired, the major affiliates became very interested in us, and in our "angle." Who was this couple who chose to speak out so boldly and publicly? What were their motives, and what was their agenda? Was this some kind of cleverly disguised political maneuver?

Some of the commentators tried to cast our position as an expression of anger against the then current administration, and the presence of U.S. troops in Iraq.

I think we were disappointing to those people. There was only one item on our agenda, and we'd stated it openly from the beginning. We had no cards up our sleeves, no secret political schemes, and no qualms with the sitting President. Beyond the obvious need for legislative action, politics didn't enter into the picture at all. Our angle was really very simple. We wanted to change a policy that governed how deceased service members were returned to American soil. That was it. Period!

Even as the story was released, John and I were making preparations to fly out to Atlanta to pick up Matthew's personal belongings and his truck. We also wanted to visit several of his close friends and his girlfriend who had flown to San Diego for his services.

By the time our plane landed in Atlanta, our cell phones were crammed with voice mails from Salvador. The national media had picked up the story over the weekend, and it seemed like every journalist in America wanted to do an interview with us. Shortly after speaking with Salvador we were inundated with calls from CNN, Fox News, MSNBC, ABC, CBS, as well as major newspapers and several freelance journalists. The week that followed was a whirlwind of interviews with the national media.

Everyone was gracious, expressing sympathy and encouragement. Through the middle of it all ran a strong thread of disbelief. The journalists didn't doubt our story, but many of them were clearly shocked to learn that our experience was not some rare exception or oversight on the part of the military. It was routine everyday policy. Deceased American heroes were being treated like bulk cargo on a daily basis, with no semblance of the honor that their sacrifices had earned.

The government was completely unprepared for the media frenzy that our first interview had triggered. Government representatives suddenly found themselves at the center of a rapidly escalating controversy, and not one of them was prepared to speak about the issue we had raised. One government spokesperson after another declined to comment. They were either completely unaware of the policy in question, or they were not willing to respond without additional research.

John and I were surprised at how quickly we had overcome the first challenge. We had ignited a firestorm and elevated the problem to national attention. So far, so good, but what could we do next?

We were grieving parents and concerned citizens, not political strategists. We realized that we had to follow up with our next step, but we had no idea what to do. Luckily, God knew exactly what we should do.

While we were still in Georgia we received a call from our pastor, Jim Baize. He had seen the coverage in San Diego, and he was checking to see how we were holding up. Prior to leaving San Diego, he had offered to coordinate a meeting with Congressman Duncan Hunter to discuss our concerns. He reiterated the offer on the phone that day.

John and I agreed. We promised to contact Pastor Baize when we returned to San Diego, so that he could set up a meeting with Congressman Hunter.

When we hung up the phone, I think John and I both felt a little better. We still couldn't see the end of our journey or how we would get there. But God had illuminated our next step on the path. All we had to do was put one foot forward.

The Holley Provision

_____

John:

Never in our wildest dreams did we ever think there would come a day when anyone would question our love of country or call us un-American. And yet when we decided to speak out — to right what we felt was a terrible wrong — that's exactly what some people did.

Just one week after laying Matthew to rest and after much discussion, I reached out to the media to share — the "story." Our intention was to raise awareness and to correct an injustice that we felt could easily be addressed if the powers that be simply understood the error of their ways. I vividly recalled the knock on our front door on that typical Southern California day in early December 2005. As we opened the door, there stood Salvador Rivera and Mike Gleeson from 10 News, the local ABC affiliate in San Diego. Both gentlemen had attended our son's military honors service just one week before. Salvador had extended his business card to me and indicated that he would be willing and ready to share our thoughts with the community of San Diego whenever we were ready to talk about the story behind the story.

So on a clear and beautiful Friday, we sat down to discuss our concerns. During the interview process Mr. Rivera was courteous and respectful in gathering the information that he felt would be needed to present our story in the proper light. That evening on the 5:00 o'clock news, the story was released as one of the main headliners. The coverage respectfully outlined our concerns and our desire to make changes to the practice of returning the remains of an American fallen hero to their loved ones. Almost immediately following the release of the news story, there were inferences made by some in the media that tried to associate us with the anti-war movement.

Nothing was further from the truth. Innuendos were made which questioned our patriotism and our support of the U.S. military.

Even as each year passes since the signing of the legislation that implemented the law surrounding The Holley Provision, it boggles our minds how anyone could have listened to our story and reached such an unfounded conclusion.

We were just everyday Americans who came from humble beginnings and used our God given talents to pursue the American dream, and to make a comfortable life for our family. We raised Matthew with Christian values and simple life lessons, amongst those, "to do unto others as you would have them do unto you." When Matthew came to us and shared his desire to serve our country and to follow in the footsteps of so many in our family, we couldn't help but swell with patriotic pride.

Un-American? The very idea was so far from reality that it should have been funny. But it wasn't funny to us. It hurt to read those comments, or hear people say such things about us. And yet, in some strange way, it gave us the encouragement to press on. As Americans we had chosen to take a stand and more importantly to exercise an important right in voicing our opinion and proposing a solution. At that point, more than ever we needed to follow through. We needed to carry the flag forward and do for others what they didn't know how to do for themselves. Thus, to venture into a public arena that we weren't even sure how to traverse.

In those early days we caught ourselves wondering how we could be any more un-American than those who stood on street corners demeaning the support of the war effort. They called our President and our military service member's baby killers in one sentence and professed to support our troops in another. What an oxymoron. How un-American was that?

As I reflect back, it's not difficult to think of perhaps a single point in time in which Matthew first considered the thought of joining the military. As many in our generation, we'll forever remember that fateful Tuesday in 2001 when those prominent twin towers fell in the New York City skyline. Matthew was just one week short of his 17th birthday, but that day was as much a catalyst for his decision to serve our nation as any. Matthew saw the cause for freedom and all he had been raised to believe in, challenged, and he expressed that if there was one thing worse than dying, it was being alive and not being free.

We knew then, although perhaps silently hoping not, that we had raised a warrior who even in those teenage years understood the true meaning of our flag, our freedoms and the foundation on which our great land was founded. He also understood that on that fateful day there was an attempt to crack our nation's foundation to expose a weakness and to rip apart the heart of a people.

Some have argued that Iraq or Afghanistan weren't our fights to fight, and yet many would argue why not? Like it or not, terrorism became our fight long, long before we ever asked for it. In the end there were really only two choices, fight them on their ground or fight them on ours. Quite frankly I'm not sure our nation could have handled, or even desired to handle such a fight on American soil. One could argue that we had many more options. Negotiation perhaps was an option. However, if one was truly honest, it would be just as fair to argue that it's nearly impossible to negotiate with a person or persons who had made it very clear that they were out to destroy those who do not share in their beliefs.

So it was by staring adversity straight on and with a marked determination in our hearts that we embarked on changing a United States federal law in the midst of a day and age when our nation was at war. Treating our fallen heroes with anything other than the utmost honor and dignity due them was the furthest thing from the minds of the nation's people. A news release seemed as good a place to start as any; and start we did.

The news story by Salvador Rivera started the ball rolling, and within forty-eight hours we learned that both national and international affiliates had picked up the story. The momentum continued. The day after the story was released we were on a plane headed to Atlanta, Georgia. Our mission was to pick up Matthew's personal belongings, which included his pick-up truck that he had left with friends prior to his deployment.

Upon landing in Atlanta we quickly learned that the story had truly taken on a life of its own. On Sunday morning I received a phone call from Salvador. He told us that 10 News had been contacted by representatives of several national news agencies who wanted to sit down and talk. He needed my permission to give them my phone number. This would continue the effort to get the word out about the treatment of our fallen heroes when returned home to their loved ones. It was a point of critical decision for us, and the answer was simple — Yes!

Stacey:

No sooner had John given the go-ahead then the phone began to ring. First came a request to speak on CNN during the Kyra Phillips show. Next would be a call from MSNBC for an interview with Keith Olbermann and then a request from Fox News to discuss our concerns on the Hannity and Colmes show. In between those calls we received requests from ABC, CBS, radio and newspaper affiliates across the country, as well as a few freelance writers.

From what we both recall, the next several days were a whirlwind of discussions, and in amongst all of that John became ill, worn down from the whole experience of Matthew's death, the funeral services, traveling back east and now the requests for us to share our story. All of it was beginning to take its toll. Regardless though, we both pressed on because it seemed there was such a short window of opportunity to get the story out in the right light and lay the proper foundation for advocating for the change we were proposing.

I took the driver's seat to work with the different contacts and make the arrangements for where we needed to be and when. Since we were in Atlanta it only made sense to coordinate the first interview with CNN, which happened to be where their central studio was located. They made it that much easier for us when they offered to have a car service come up to the North Atlanta area where we were staying and drive us over to their studios.

Upon our arrival we were taken aback by the enormity and significance of their complex in the heart of downtown Atlanta. After waiting for our clearance and badge to access the facility, we were taken upstairs to the makeup department. Yes, it was just like you would see in the movies. Makeup, lights and cameras, up close and personal. After we were done in the makeup room, an intern came in to introduce herself. She said she would lead us over to the studio where the interview with Kyra Phillips would happen on live television. Had it not been for the circumstances, we both would have considered it one the most incredible experiences we'd ever had.

The moment was dampened slightly by the seriousness of the subject we would be sharing with the nation and yet there we were just one short week after laying our son Matthew to rest. Now we were sharing Matthew with the entire world. More importantly we had an opportunity to make an enormous impact on the families that would unfortunately follow in our footsteps in receiving the remains of their fallen hero or heroine home from the battlefield.

As we entered the studio we had a glimpse of where we would be conducting our interview. The intern led us over to an area just off the set where Ms. Phillips was finishing up with another guest. The intern informed us they would be breaking away to report on a leading story regarding former President Gerald Ford who had suffered a heart attack earlier that day. Before we knew it though, the intern was back and guiding us toward the interview platform where Ms. Phillips would be speaking with us. They prepared our mikes and made sure everything tested fine, and then told us it would be just a few more minutes.

Moments before the actual interview began Ms. Phillips began to talk with us — if anything just to calm us down. And then it was time. The producer gave us a countdown of sorts and Ms. Phillips guided us through a series of questions almost as if we were close friends. She made us feel completely at ease and allowed the both of us to share from our hearts to the world about Matthew, his love of art and karate. They showed photos of us as a family including some of the last ones John had taken just weeks before Matthew deployed to Iraq. We will be forever grateful to CNN for giving us that opportunity.

Following the interview our contact thanked us and offered to have the car service take us over to the other news affiliates that we were scheduled to speak with that evening. Their driver would also be available to drive us back to our hotel afterwards. We headed over to MSNBC where John interviewed with Keith Olbermann and then finished the evening by speaking on Fox News with Sean Hannity and Alan Colmes through a remote feed with the local Fox news affiliate. The latter two interviews were interesting. We saw how the studios were remotely controlled by personnel in their main New York locations. There was a technician locally assigned to set up the seating area and our mikes, but the camera was remotely controlled from New York and the producers gave direction from New York as well.

So much had happened around us and to us in those early days. This was yet another surreal experience. John's illness added another dimension, but we were determined not to let this chance pass us by to share what we felt to be a very important message. The proper entities in the government needed to understand that there was a more dignified and respectful way for parents to witness the arrival of their fallen hero. Loved ones should not have to see them reach their final destination being driven around a freight terminal on a forklift.

Shortly after finishing the Hannity and Colmes interview we were contacted by Allen Colmes' radio producer asking if John would call in during his radio program later that evening. In the span of a twelve hour period we had provided interviews on three major news networks, interviewed with two newspapers and a radio affiliate on the west coast, been contacted by a freelance writer for the website Military.com and ended the evening with a call into the Alan Colmes' radio show. Somewhere in between all of those interviews we both realized we couldn't turn back.

As John wrapped up the call to Alan Colmes' show, we became acutely aware we had just taken the first steps toward tackling the challenge before us. As with the others before him, Mr. Colmes was very courteous and allowed John to openly share our story. Shortly after he concluded that interview it was time to rest, and then we would need to follow through. Looking back several years later, both of us acknowledge that we will be forever grateful to each of the media groups that spoke to us in those early days and to those that conducted follow-up interviews over the course of the next year. In many ways had it not been for their encouragement The Holley Provision may not have happened.

Our trip to Atlanta concluded after about a week, having packed up Matthew's personal belongings and making the necessary arrangements to have the Army ship his truck back to San Diego. During that same week we also received another call from our pastor, Jim Baize. He called to see how we were holding up under the pressure that he could only imagine we were under. He also wanted to follow up on an offer he had extended earlier to put us in direct contact with Congressman Duncan Hunter, then the head of the Armed Services Committee of the House of Representatives. We agreed on a date and time, and waited for a follow-up call about the get-together.

Sometime the week of December 19, 2005 in a restaurant in National City, California we sat down over a cup of coffee with Mr. Hunter, Pastor Baize and his wife Pat to discuss our story. We exercised a very important right that every American citizen has, the right to express their desire to advocate for change in a law, and to see that change followed through on their behalf by those voted into office to serve the needs of their constituency.

Mr. Hunter listened to our story and asked us a very simple question, "What would you like to see happen to change the policy of how our fallen heroes are brought home?"

John outlined a process that included the journey being a military operation alone. We believed that their brothers and sisters in arms should handle our fallen heroes all the way from overseas through Dover to their home of record. Secondly, we felt that every hero should be welcomed by an honor guard of military personnel upon the arrival of their flight at the airport. The honor guard should remove the casket from the aircraft with nothing less than full honors. Third, we felt that the hero's loved ones should be allowed onto the tarmac of the airport to witness their arrival if they chose, and lastly that the casket be escorted to the final resting place by the same honor guard. All of this in difference to the casket being shipped as cargo and upon arrival at the airport offloaded by baggage handlers and fork-lifted to the freight terminal warehouse where the loved ones or funeral home personnel could pick up the casket.

The revelation of how a fallen hero's arrival had been handled was noted by one military spokesperson as being "the most expeditious way to get the remains delivered to their relatives." To which John couldn't help but respond by asking, "If it was expeditious to deliver them in *garbage trucks*, would you do that?"

In the end we conveyed to Mr. Hunter that it wasn't about being expeditious, it was about dignity, honor and utmost respect — that last measure of devotion our nation owed that hero and their parents or loved ones, as that sight would be one of the final memories that they would have.

Early on in the process John had found a picture on the Internet that reflected the arrival of a Marine hero in his casket on the forks of a forklift in a warehouse. His parents were standing there staring at this absolutely unacceptable sight. John shared that picture with Congressman Hunter as an example of what no parent or loved one should endure for their family's ultimate sacrifice. In the days that followed Mr. Hunter used that picture to share amongst his peers in Washington D.C. as an argument of why The Holley Provision was needed and the importance of such a change to legislation.

And, so it was over a cup of coffee that our desire to see a wrong righted came to be. When called upon over the next many months, we took every opportunity to conduct interviews as we were requested. We were determined to give our all, just as Matthew and all of our fallen had done to see this through. In October 2006, less than one year after we spoke from our hearts with Salvador Rivera in our San Diego home, John received a call from Mr. Hunter's Washington D.C. office. As part of the National Defense Authorization Act for Fiscal 2007, President Bush signed into law what is now known as The Holley Provision in honor of our son, Specialist Matthew John Holley.

As part of the journey to passing this important legislation, Congressman Duncan Hunter read into the Congressional Record from the House floor the following statement on the provision involving the transportation of our fallen heroes.

H.R. 5122, NATIONAL DEFENSE AUTHORIZATION ACT FOR FISCAL YEAR 2007
(House of Representatives - May 10, 2006)

The following is Representative Duncan Hunter's (R-CA) floor statement on the provision involving the transportation of our fallen Soldiers.

Mr. Hunter:

"Mr. Chairman, I just wanted to say to my colleagues that this, the story of this global war against terror with the special focus in Iraq and Afghanistan, is a story of families. It is a story of enormous sacrifice, not just by the people that wear the uniform in the theater, but by their families back home, their moms, their dads, their wives, their husbands, their children.

And there is a particular family, the Holley family from San Diego, California, that brought an issue to the attention of the Armed Services Committee here over this last year when their great 101st Airborne Trooper, Matthew Holley, was killed in the Iraq theater. And they pointed out that in the present chain of transportation of our fallen heroes home, where they come through Dover, Delaware, and ultimately go to their final resting place at their particular hometown or community in America, that part of that chain of transportation has been carried out by commercial airlines. And despite the best wishes and the best efforts on the part of those people who operate the commercial airlines, the proper amount of respect, the extreme respect that should be afforded those fallen heroes is in some cases, has in some cases been lacking.

And that came to the attention of the Holley family. And they talked to me and to other members of the committee, and we looked at the issue and as a result of that, we have, in the law, in this bill or in the proposed law, some very clear and strong directives to the administration to utilize military aircraft in taking our fallen heroes from Dover, Delaware, from where they land on American shores, to the military base that is closest to their hometown, unless otherwise directed by the family, and to use those military aircraft and to accompany those fallen heroes with American military personnel, and to greet that military aircraft when it arrives at that military base closest to their hometown with an honor guard.

And so we have laid out very directive language, very clear language for the administration. And I want to thank John and Stacy, who really brought this to our attention in honor of their son, Matthew Holley. And I think that we have talked to the other body and I think that this will have clear support all the way through.

But this is an important part of this bill because part of this bill is about respect. And this particular provision is about respect for those people who have given that last full measure of devotion to our country.

Mr. Chairman, I yield back the balance of my time."

The Holley Provision in action, properly preparing for the welcome home of a fallen American hero.

From our original discussion with Mr. Hunter in a restaurant in December 2005, to the final version of the legislation, little changed. Today every American fallen hero is flown to the airport closest to their home of record on a small military charter jet, by military transport or via commercial airlines. The rest of our requests were completely honored. Upon the arrival of a fallen American hero, the casket is met by an honor guard in crisp uniforms and white gloves, to be witnessed by family members. We will be forever grateful and thankful to all the men and women who through their care and concern to have our story told, helped to effect the change that is now known as The Holley Provision.

A Journey of Grief

John:

It was the best of times; it was the worst of times... I sometimes wonder if Charles Dickens sensed that his words were destined to become one of the most recognizable passages in English literature, when he wrote the opening lines to *A Tale of Two Cities*. I've come across those lines many times in my life, and until recently I recognized them as nothing more than a classic literary reference. But I seem to be running into those words more often these days, and they've taken on a whole new meaning for me.

It was the best of times; it was the worst of times... In many ways, that seems to sum things up for me. Somehow, in the midst of pain, Stacey and I have begun to find purpose. Even as one path to our future has been closed off, we are finding new paths that lead us forward.

In many ways my trip to Iraq was an expedition into the very heart of my grief. It was a chance to travel to the land where Matthew gave his life and to walk upon the very soil where he had walked. It was an opportunity filled with promise and pain. *It was the best of times; it was the worst of times...*

April 2006

It popped up without warning. I was talking to Stacey on the phone, and she mentioned finding a link to a website about Gold Star parents traveling to Iraq. The idea instantly seized my attention, and I began firing off questions. Who was sponsoring the trip? When were they leaving? How could we get in touch with them?

For the first time since losing Matthew, I felt energized and focused. Stacey had just come across the link, and she hadn't been able to follow up with any research yet. All she had was a phone number.

That was enough for me. I dialed the number immediately after I hung up from her call. To my disappointment no one answered. I left a message explaining who I was, and asking for someone to contact me as soon as possible to discuss the details of the trip.

71

The wheels were already spinning in my head. I had to go. I didn't know how the parents would be selected for the trip, but I knew that I needed to be among them. Every fiber of my being was screaming at me to find a way.

My brain began running through every possibility, no matter how crazy. I thought again about re-enlisting in the Army and shipping over as a Soldier. I knew that Duncan Hunter was planning a trip to Iraq, and I tried to figure out if it might be possible to stow away on his plane.

Whatever it took, I had to travel to Iraq. I had to stare down the anonymous enemy that had murdered my son, to pick up Matthew's fallen flag and continue on into battle.

Even now, several years later, those feelings in me are still strong. You've heard the old saying, "like father, like son." If those words had ever been true, they were true for Matthew and me. He had followed in my footsteps to become a warrior. Now, it was time for me to walk in *his* footsteps.

That first day no one returned my call. By the time I crawled into bed, I was jumping at anything that sounded like a ringing phone.

Another day passed, and still no one called. I had exhausted my patience, so I dialed the number again. As before, there was no answer. I left another message.

This time, I received a call back. I explained to the gentleman on the other end of the phone that I was a Gold Star parent, and I asked if he was familiar with the media blitz surrounding The Holley Provision. The gentleman assured me that he was quite familiar with the story.

He proceeded to take down some information about me and as we concluded the call, I insisted that he put my name on the list. As I recall, I got rather pushy about it. Looking back, I hope I wasn't rude to the gentleman. If I was, I hope he will accept my sincere apologies. I needed to go to Iraq. That's all I thought about.

The gentleman assured me that he had all the information he needed and promised to get back in touch.

As I mentioned earlier, some of the details have become a little fuzzy, but I do remember that I was asked to help raise funds for the trip by conducting a number of telethon-style radio interviews. I participated in several interviews of this sort, sharing our story and talking about Matthew. The details of the interviews varied, but the core issues were always the same. We talked about Matthew's decision to serve our nation, and his determination to make a difference in the world. We also talked about the work that Stacey and I were doing with the legislation.

Things continued in this general pattern from April 2006 until late October 2006, when I received another phone call.

October 2006

No matter how fuzzy my memory becomes, I don't think I will ever forget that phone conversation. It was the same guy, the gentleman who had returned my call the previous April. We'd talked on the phone a number of times since that first call, but this time was different.

After exchanging the usual greetings, he came straight to the point. "Do you still want to go to Iraq?"

I didn't hesitate for even a millisecond. "Of course, I do!"

"Okay," he said. "You're still not guaranteed to go, but hold tight. I'll get back to you with an answer in the next day or two."

My heart nearly stopped. I had been waiting six months for an answer, and suddenly the idea of waiting another day or two seemed impossible. I couldn't even imagine waiting that long.

Luckily, I didn't have to. The call came the very next day. The phone rang, and the gentleman got right to the point. "You're a go!"

I was positively ecstatic. There were a lot of details to figure out, but none of that mattered. I was going!

The gentleman on the other end of the phone then informed me that we had not received permission or assistance from the U.S. Government. Uncle Sam wasn't going to hinder our trip, but he wasn't going to help either.

Plan "B" was to leverage contacts that had been established with the Kurdish government in Northern Iraq. Due to this change in approach, it was imperative to keep the timing and details of our travel plans a secret for security reasons. I was completely comfortable with the request for secrecy. My phone contact, the gentleman I had been working with since April, was a United States Marine Gunnery Sergeant reservist. He had been to Iraq, and he was well versed in the required security measures.

To some degree, I was, too. During my time as a Military Policeman in the U.S. Army, I had held a top-secret security clearance. Those years were long behind me, but I hadn't forgotten the importance of operational security.

The last thing we wanted to do was give the terrorists advance notice that a group of Gold Star parents were headed into Iraq's war zone. If any harm came to us, it would be a huge media coup for the enemy's cause, not to mention a severe blow to the United States government and to our deployed service members. *Parents Of Fallen Heroes Lose Their Lives In*

Iraq. None of us wanted a headline like that. The Gunnery Sergeant and I discussed a few more details about the trip, and then hung up the phone. It was time to tell Stacey that I had received the green light.

She and I had already been preparing for a trip to Fort Campbell where the 101st Airborne Division 2nd Brigade was holding a remembrance ceremony to honor their fallen brothers. Matthew had deployed to Iraq with that unit, so I found myself with a bit of a dilemma. Should I make the trip to Kentucky with Stacey? Or should I embark on the trip to Iraq?

To be honest, dilemma is probably too strong a word. I knew that I would choose Iraq, but my heart was still torn.

When I finally connected with Stacey, I informed her that I had been approved for the trip to Iraq. I really wanted to go, but it was only fair to ask for her consent. If she gave me the green light, she would have to attend the ceremony at Fort Campbell without me. More importantly, it meant risking another member of our family in the very place where we had lost our son.

Deep down, I believe Stacey knew and understood my need to go to Iraq. This might well be the only chance I would ever get. With reluctance, and I'm certain more than a little hidden fear, she gave me the go-ahead.

I called my contact back within two hours and gave him all the information he needed to make travel arrangements. As I hung up the phone, reality began to sink in. In less than one week I would be traveling to Iraq with several Gold Star parents — some of whom I had never met. It was really happening. For good or for ill, we were headed to one of the most dangerous countries in the world.

I began thinking about another trip I had made to San Diego's Lindbergh Field several years earlier. That date was September 11, 2001.

It had started out as a normal business trip. I was scheduled to fly out of San Diego to close a real estate deal in North Idaho. As she often did, Stacey offered to take me to the airport that day. We never arrived.

A few minutes into our short drive to the airport, the car radio sounded the emergency broadcast warning system. Normally we would have ignored such a notice. But that morning was different.

We listened in growing horror to the unfathomable news. The World Trade Center towers in New York had been attacked, and the United States air traffic system was being completely shut down.

Like many other Americans, we spent the remainder of that day watching every scrap of available news, in complete disbelief that such a heinous act had been perpetrated against thousands of innocent civilians.

Still stunned, Stacey and I drove back to the airport the next morning to see about the possibility of flying north. It was a dreary, overcast day, and the airport was like a ghost town. In place of the usual bustle of cars and people, we encountered emptiness and silence. The nature of the world had shifted somehow, and we didn't yet understand how profound that change had been.

As Stacey dropped me at the airport curb on September 12, even the air seemed different. The unexpected quiet was almost surreal. We didn't talk much, but Stacey got out of the car with me as I went to the trunk for my bags. The terrorist assault that we now refer to as 9/11 was only twenty-four hours old.

In keeping with our family tradition, Stacey and I exchanged hugs and thumbs along with our usual sign for I love you. We had no way of knowing at that time that just a short four years later the events of the previous day would lead our son to the other side of the world. Matthew would go to Iraq to combat terrorism in one of the strongholds of oppression. And one day, I would follow him.

As I walked through the glass doors of the San Diego airport on that September morning in 2001, I had no idea I was taking the very first step of my journey to Iraq.

The Iraq Pack

John:

San Diego, California

I was a bit nervous as I watched Stacey drive away from the airport unloading zone on that cool November morning in 2006. Of course, there were nerves. I was about to embark on a journey to the land where our son had taken his last breath of life. A life taken far too early and far short of his potential. To put it simply, I was walking into a precarious, possibly dangerous situation in a very perilous part of the world. Yet as day one of the journey was underway, I felt it was worth the risk to seek answers to those unspoken questions that I and those traveling with me had. Ultimately, were the sacrifices our children made really worth our loss?

Nerves aside, I stepped inside the terminal to go through the formalities of checking in at the ticket counter to begin what would turn out to be a twenty-four-hour travel day. After clearing security I waited another hour before boarding the flight to Chicago. As I headed down the jetway to the plane I went through a process, some would say a ritual, to bless the plane and my journey. With the passengers settled in, the plane departed San Diego on time around 8:20 a.m. with a scheduled arrival in Chicago four hours later.

Chicago, Illinois

For the most part there was nothing unusual about the first leg of my trip. We were still in the United States, and in general I felt safe. I was seated next to a very nice woman who I learned was born and raised in Iran, and was now living in San Diego. She happened to be heading to Iran to visit relatives. Being acutely aware of raising any red flags regarding my travel plans and the security situation surrounding them, I chose not to discuss the details surrounding my final destination. As we arrived in Chicago I wished her safe travels and deplaned. I made my way over to the

77

international terminal to meet up with the rest of the group that I would travel with on Royal Jordanian Airlines.

In a strange way we were members of an exclusive club — a club none of us would ever have willingly joined. We were Gold Star parents, parents of children who had given the ultimate sacrifice in service to their nation. As is often my habit when gathering in groups, I quickly gave us a name — "The Iraq Pack." It reminded me of the "Rat Pack" from the 50s, and in terms of the journey we were about to embark on, I felt the name appropriate.

Also traveling with us were two members of Move America Forward, the organization that had helped to coordinate our travel arrangements. They would also coordinate schedules and appointments with various personnel once we arrived in Iraq. In addition, we had a reporter traveling with us to capture and provide insight on various aspects of our journey. I sensed immediately that everyone was upbeat and excited, and ready to embark on our passage. Over the next several hours while we waited to board our flight to Jordan, we became better acquainted than a few emails or phone calls had allowed us to do over the past several months. As it turned out we ended up spending an additional three hours on the ground than originally intended. The inbound flight and follow-on preparation for the trip to Jordan had been delayed. We departed Chicago at approximately 9 p.m. with an estimated arrival time into Amman, Jordan at 8:15 p.m. Jordanian time — eleven hours later.

Prior to taking this trip I had traveled internationally — even since 9/11 — and I recall nothing especially different about this flight, with one exception. Almost immediately upon boarding I noticed a gentleman that I determined was most likely an on-board security person or international sky marshal. I came to that conclusion because throughout the boarding process he randomly stepped out from behind a forward partition. He wore a suit and tie, and appeared fit. His hair and mustache were dark. His eyes were hidden under very dark sunglasses. Each time he stepped from behind the partition he looked straight at me.

I wasn't necessarily concerned, but I couldn't help wonder why in the world he was staring at me. Then it occurred to me that I must have looked suspicious to him because I, too, was wearing very dark sunglasses. It wasn't unusual for me to have sunglasses on when I traveled. Not only did I use them outdoors, but over the years I had become accustomed to wearing them to help calm me and for sleeping on the plane. In most instances I was the only one wearing sunglasses, but considering the region of the world we were traveling to, I must have made his spidey senses tingle. I tried to ignore him and prepare myself for what would be a very long flight — destination Amman, Jordan!

Amman, Jordan

As we deplaned we were now literally within hours of our final destination. We were required to go through a process of purchasing visas and then proceed through the normal customs process.

Those initial memories of Amman were almost surreal in nature. Because of the lateness of our arrival, the airport was fairly empty. As we retrieved our luggage I noticed warmth in the air. Perhaps I shouldn't have been so surprised. We were in an arid desert part of the world. I suppose because of the time of the year, I expected a cooler temperature. With luggage in hand, we stepped outside into an eerie pitch-black night. As my eyes adjusted I noticed an orange and yellow glow from the outdoor lights, a distinct glow that even to this day I remember. It just seemed dreamlike. Was I really doing this? Was I literally within 600 miles of Iraq?

No longer were we focused on the formality of entering a foreign country. I began taking in our immediate surroundings. As I looked around outside the terminal I honed in on the Arabic signs. There were also signs in English, but seeing the Arabic signs confirmed that I was that much closer to Iraq. The organization that coordinated our travel arrangements had scheduled a small bus to pick us up, but as we stepped to the curb there was no bus to be found. One of our chaperones left us and rejoined the group about ten minutes later having secured alternative transportation in the form of small taxis. I wasn't quite sure how official they were, but that's what we had.

Our new drivers pulled their vehicles up to the curbside and began loading our luggage into the trunks of the various cars. The team quickly recognized that not all the bags were going to fit, and as if knowing they would have to improvise, out came strands of rope. Obviously they were prepared to handle such circumstances. They proceeded to pile the remaining bags on the roofs of the cars, tying them down for our ride to the hotel. Needless to say, my bag ended up being one of those tied to a rooftop, and so I waited on the curb, paying close attention to ensure it was properly secure. At that late hour half way around the world, the only thing going through my mind despite being hungry and tired was envisioning the contents of my bag strewn all over a Jordanian highway. After I had satisfied myself that my bag, along with the others, was safely secure, I squeezed my not-so-small frame into a car and off we went into the darkness.

We exited the airport and out onto a poorly lit highway. Oh how I wished for the luxuries of safety we enjoy in the United States. As we drove along we occasionally came upon another vehicle, but with a honk of the driver's horn, we passed. I recall a sense of uneasiness about the whole situation. I hoped that our journey ended well with the group arriving at the hotel as scheduled. I thought maybe we were being setup. Were the drivers American-friendly and in fact taking us to our hotel? Or were we on an ominous detour being driven into the desert where we would be handed over to a terrorist organization for exploitation and perhaps even execution.

I know that's a little dramatic, but I'm sure similar thoughts were on the minds of the other Gold Star parents. Mainly since the media was front and center that Americans traveling to or living in foreign countries, especially in the Middle and Near East, faced danger. Thoughts of foreigner's taken hostage in places like the Philippines, Somalia, Iran and Pakistan raced through my mind. Imagine for a moment the scene. We were a group of ten Americans whizzing down a highway in a region of the world where many wished harm upon and targeted groups such as ours.

We continued racing down that highway in the pitch-black night occasionally honking and passing, honking and passing. There were highway signs, and in some small way they comforted me even though I had no true sense of where we were or even where we would end up. I remember thinking that if anything did happen before arriving at the hotel, I was prepared to fight. I would not go down easily.

In what seemed like forever, but in actuality was more like thirty minutes, we began to see signs of civilization — more lights and buildings as we neared the city center. With a continued heightened sense for anything out of the ordinary, we were happy when our convoy of cars slowed and turned into a driveway. Our hotel was now in view. Safety at last — and relief in knowing that we would be okay.

Then everything blurred again. I remember a brightly lighted doorway. It was still very dark, and I couldn't make out much of anything else. It's almost as if after such a long trip I had complete tunnel vision. The group, with the help of the drivers, unloaded our bags. Our sponsors paid the drivers and finally we stepped inside the hotel. But right before the group could enter complete safety we found ourselves passing through another airport-style security checkpoint. Our luggage was placed one piece at a time onto a conveyor belt so it could be x-rayed for explosives and weapons. Then we passed through metal detectors, and finally were inside in a place of calm and safety for the next twenty-four hours.

I proceeded to check-in, picked up my room key and headed for the elevator, all the while taking in our surroundings and especially noting the beautiful decor of the hotel. I dropped off my bag in the room, splashed some cold water on my face and headed back down to meet the others in the hotel restaurant. As I stepped into the restaurant I couldn't believe it. I had just traveled halfway around the world, leaving San Diego, California, the home of the best Mexican cuisine outside of Mexico, and where do I end up for my first meal in the Middle East? A Mexican restaurant! How ironic was that? I must admit the food was pretty good.

We sat there eating and blowing off steam — nervous about attracting too much attention to our group. Many of us spoke in lowered voices and tried to avoid language that might offend anyone who had a negative view of Americans. After about an hour I stood to excuse myself. I bid goodnight to all and made my way back to my room. I cleaned up, changed clothes, crawled into bed and promptly fell asleep. I was exhausted, and rest was a necessity. Tomorrow would be a big day — a day that would end poorly for me.

The Attack

John:

Friday morning I awoke to my new surroundings. Once again I found myself contemplating the enormity of this journey and the meaning it offered each of the parents who were selected to travel to Iraq — to the land where our young heroes gave their last measure of devotion for the protection of our nation.

As I was getting ready to go downstairs and meet up with the rest of the group in the restaurant, I took a few moments to glance out my bedroom window. It seemed to be like any other large city around the world. I quickly realized it was not. I was in Amman, Jordan and in many ways the scenery was much different from anything I had ever seen before. I finished getting ready and headed downstairs to connect with the rest of our group.

I found them already seated around a large round table in a private area towards the back of the restaurant. Laid out before us was quite the spread of eggs, potatoes, fresh fruit, pastries, juices etc… As would become the norm over the next several days, there was a fair amount of small talk as we ate. It was apparent that we were all experiencing some level of jet lag. Yet at the same time we were excited about the activities for our day and what lay beyond. The next day we would arrive at our main destination — Iraq! On this day though, we were tourists.

With breakfast complete, we headed outside to see some of the local attractions. Our first jaunt would be to a Roman amphitheatre. We shared a natural concern and reservation as our plan required us to walk through the streets of Amman to get to our destination. Based on what we had learned prior to departing the hotel, the walk would be at least two miles. As we had no guide with us, we weren't quite sure where we were headed. Under normal circumstances I'm not one who likes to go anywhere without a well thought-out plan, but I threw caution to the wind as I was about to fulfill a lifelong dream of exploring a Roman ruin. I was more than game.

So off we went, nine somewhat intrepid explorers under the bright blue sky of Amman. As we stepped outside of the hotel we were greeted by an absolutely beautiful day, clear skies and temperate conditions. Wow! We literally stood in the middle of the city. Due to the late arrival at the hotel the night before, we'd been unsure exactly where we were. Immediately I noticed two large hotels close by, each centered on a large traffic circle that appeared to be a central point of the city. Most buildings were some shade of white. Across the way off a short distance we saw a rather large mosque with a beautiful blue dome and two minarets. Under the bright sky it was a very striking structure. I recalled seeing this scene back home watching TV as it was often the backdrop for many news reports in the U.S. How cool to see it in person.

After taking a few pictures of the mosque we headed off in the direction of the ruins. I quickly noticed our group was alone, as there was virtually no one else on the streets. We were surrounded by an interesting mixture of ancient architecture amongst newer buildings, in addition to some rather rundown structures. As I glanced off into the distance there were a variety of Arabic billboards and pictures of King Hussein, along with a rather large sign promoting Rolex watches. I'm not sure why, but that seemed especially interesting to me. As I continued to look around I noticed another building off in the distance. It was a little smaller than those surrounding it, but the Christian cross on top caught my eye. I assumed it was a church, which both amazed and brought a sense of comfort to me. In an area of the world where conflict was driven by the distinct differences in the people's beliefs, different religious icons peacefully co-existed side by side. *Surreal*, to say the least.

As our group continued walking we came upon another familiar sight — a Mobil gas station. And as we took in our surroundings, one of the others called my attention to a small well-worn truck that happened to be stopped at the curb. They pointed to a U.S. license plate from Mississippi. Of course, I took a picture.

As we continued on our journey we passed by a person here and there. Thinking back, I'm sure they were caught off guard by nine Caucasian Americans casually out for a stroll through their town. Near one of the buildings we passed, we noticed a gentleman about three stories up on his balcony smoking a hookah pipe, carefully watching us. As we passed by I caught a glimpse of him pulling his cell phone out of his pocket to make a call, all the while continuing to keep an eye on us. Reflecting back it turned out to be nothing, but considering the part of the world we were in at the time my intuition was telling me to be aware. Expect the best, but remain alert — again a reminder of the region of the world we were visiting.

We continued walking toward the ruins, stopping to rest, taking pictures and checking our bearings, again noticing how few people were outside. Finally, as we neared the bottom of the hill leading to the amphitheater, people began to appear, slowly at first and then suddenly the streets were crowded. We learned later that Friday in Amman is their Holy Day or the equivalent of our Sabbath, with the first part of the day dedicated to prayer. During this period virtually no one ventures out of doors, nor do they conduct business.

As the crowds grew around us, it became apparent that we were noticed. While most of those around us were expressionless, I remember one gentleman who didn't look very happy that we were out walking around. Most people though, just kept moving past, more interested in conducting their own business. We arrived at the bottom of the hill, pausing on the corner to decide whether to go left or right to find the Roman ruins. Feeling a little uncomfortable and still very much out of place, not wanting to stand still for very long, we chose to go to the right. We moved slowly along the sidewalk observing the vendors selling their wares. Across the street I noticed what appeared to be a very old mosque, brown in color and definitely showing the wear of its lifetime. Snap goes the camera as we continue on our trek once again, stopping briefly to get our bearings and venture on.

Without warning, just as I was about to step off the curb to cross the street, I was startled by a small explosion. Already on edge by being caught up in a crowd, I looked at myself to see if I was bleeding or if I had any holes in me that shouldn't be there. After a second or two I found I still had all my parts and I wasn't bleeding. Out of the corner of my eye I noticed a young boy laughing in our direction. Behind him was a small group of younger boys and a few teenagers. It appeared we were their entertainment for the day. I assume the small explosion was a firework of some sort. I wasn't amused, and I'm sure the look I gave conveyed that.

Our group re-assembled and made the decision to head back to the point where we had turned right and instead took the left turn. In short order we were at the amphitheatre. We had been very near when we made the wrong turn. Oh, well. We made it to our desired location to gaze upon the Amphitheatre. I thought, *how awesome is this?*

After a lifetime of dreaming about such a moment, I was about to explore a Roman ruin. As we descended on the amphitheater everyone took several pictures from outside the fence that surrounded the ruins. In front of us were large blocks of stone with Roman writing chiseled into them. How fabulous! We made our way to the entrance gate where we were met by a brusque elderly gentleman, small in stature.

After negotiating our fee for a guided tour he waved his hand directing us to get moving. I found him quite hilarious. Instead of being guided, it felt as if we were being herded along. As we walked we'd occasionally stop, and in his best English our guide told us the importance of this or that. Then when he was ready, he would point and wave for us to follow him. At one point he even said, "Make it snappy," making the group of us laugh. It was great.

As we were guided around the amphitheater I took note of a few things that I wanted to do in the outside performance area. I separated from the rest of the group to climb the stairs to the top of the stadium seating. What a climb! As I viewed the landscape from the top seating area I correlated it to the nosebleed seats of the Roman era. I descended the steps and stopped to sit on what appeared to be a throne. Perhaps I sat in the seat reserved for a very important person from a time long, long ago. It represented an opportunity for another photo op.

One of the most interesting things that our guide showed the group was in the main performance area of the Amphitheatre. As we closed in on the area we noticed there was a very distinct "X" carved into the floor. In days of old the "X" indicated the best place for the orator to stand in order to be heard by the entire audience. I found this amazing. Our guide shared that by the orator choosing to stand on the center of the "X", those in the highest seats could hear the performer and the accentuation in the acoustics were the best from that point as well.

As our tour neared the end our guide led us out a different gate from where we had entered, which deposited us directly outside the complex near the opening to a very rustic tourist shop. As a courtesy, the group went inside and looked around at the local items. Some of them bought souvenirs, but I chose to save my money for the bazaars once we were in Iraq. Slowly the group gathered back together outside the shop. We stood around resting from our long walk and talking about heading back to the hotel for a nap as most of us were still experiencing some level of jet lag. Before a nap though, we would have to tackle the trek back up that hill to the hotel. The walk down had been all right, but the trek up looked rather daunting, not to mention by now our feet were very tired. Perhaps he sensed our concern, because our guide flagged down a couple of cabs to drive us back up the hill. We gladly hopped into several taxis and within minutes we were back at the hotel — *Hallelujah*!

Upon arrival at our hotel we again passed through the metal detectors and headed up to our rooms for an afternoon nap, agreeing to meet back in the hotel lounge area later that evening to discuss the next part of our journey. The nap was just what I needed, and after about an hour and a half of sleep I woke up feeling much rested. I headed to the hotel buffet to grab a bite to eat. After finishing my meal, I ordered my usual cup of coffee and went to the lounge where I met up with the others.

For the next couple of hours we sat around shooting the breeze, talking about our day's events and looking forward to the next day's journey that would take us across the border into Iraq. As our conversation continued I began to notice my stomach starting to feel a bit queasy and unsettled. Initially I tried to ignore the feelings, but eventually it became very uncomfortable so I excused myself and headed back to my room. In the short time it took for me to go from the lounge to my room, I began feeling worse and by the time I had entered my room I knew I was in serious trouble. My stomach became very hard and bloated and then the nausea began. I felt as if I was literally going to explode. I was in extreme distress, to the point I began asking God to allow me to vomit. For the next several hours it was bad. Within minutes my prayer was answered and the relief came in bouts. I felt like I was Godzilla in one of his movies I didn't realize that although my prayer had been answered, worse feelings were yet to come. Back in my Army days I'd had a bout with food poisoning, but this particular episode was far worse than anything I had ever experienced or care to ever experience again.

Once the vomiting stopped, I changed my clothes and lay down to get some rest. The bloating was gone from my stomach, but I still had a horrible feeling of nausea. The symptoms took another course into a new phase with the onslaught of a fever, something like I had never felt before. I began to wonder if I might actually die. For the next six hours I laid in bed writhing in pain, tossing and turning in a pool of sweat, getting little if any sleep. I kept watch on the clock to see how long I had until I had to get up to get ready for the flight to Iraq. And, yes it did cross my mind several times whether or not I should call someone to help me. In the end I decided against doing so because I had come much too far to not step foot into Iraq. No way I would turn back now.

I considered my options and knew if I was mortally ill I could be treated at an Army facility in Iraq rather than in a hospital in Jordan. I must accomplish the goal I had set for myself shortly after Matthew's death. I needed to set my feet on the soil where Matthew gave his life, the soil of Iraq. I was far too close to have that honor taken from me. As each hour passed it seemed like an eternity, and then it was 5 a.m. As quickly as the onslaught of the past six hours of pain had arrived, my fever broke and I uttered out loud to myself, "Thank God, I'm going to make it. I'm going to Iraq!"

Iraq At Last!

John:

I willed myself out of bed that morning to take a shower and pack my belongings. I was in a state of extreme exhaustion and weakness. I had just spent a horrible night fighting a virus and feeling as if a Mack truck had run me over. It took every bit of energy I could muster to slog my way downstairs and meet up with the rest of our group. I was very thankful that my fever had broken and I was no longer in agonizing pain. The residual effects of aching all over and the weak feelings that followed would be something I'd have to deal with — after all I was so very close — there was simply no way I would be denied a place on the next step of our journey!

While the others chatted during breakfast, I chimed in to ask if any of them had fallen ill during the evening, to which they replied, "No." Breakfast or not, I had to share my episode from the night before, and my rendition of the story brought a roar of laughter. What can I say — it was a perfect opportunity to make lemonade from lemons. I couldn't understand why no one else had come down with the same virus. I thought my illness must have stemmed from something I had eaten at the buffet. I was still pretty weak and had no desire to eat anything so instead chose to drink some juice. I needed to boost my energy and get something into my body. As it turned out, my appetite for the remainder of the trip would be so damaged from that overnight ordeal that I ate very little. Ultimately when I returned to the United States and jumped on the scale I was ten pounds lighter.

Eventually it was time for everyone to leave to catch the flight into Iraq. Once again we piled into several small taxis and headed back to the Amman airport. This time we were able to get a glimpse of the sites we'd missed on the way to the hotel just a couple of nights before. As we sped along it was clear that Amman, Jordan was in a desert region of the world. Everything was brown.

As we arrived at the airport terminal, we were met by baggage handlers at the curb who showed their eagerness to assist us. So much so, that they verbalized the term "tips" and went about the process of piling our bags onto a luggage cart.

Once our luggage was secure we were whisked to and fro throughout the airport until we arrived at an access point distinctly marked "Pilots and Crews Only." What ensued over the next several minutes was quite hilarious. The baggage handlers tried to gain entrance by attempting to pull the luggage cart with our bags through a set of restricted access doors. All the while they were attempting to get the cart through the area, they were being told by security personnel on the other side that they could not enter. Even so, they continued with persistence, and one could only imagine the words being exchanged by the body language being used during this tug-of war.

While this was going on, many other travelers who were obviously not pilots or crewmembers were passing through that same access point. By all appearances it was who you knew, or the money you were willing to delve out for the gatekeeper that determined whether you could pass through or not.

Finally, appearing rebuffed, our baggage handlers cut over into a much longer line so that our group and bags could pass through security and then get into yet another line to check in for our flight. As we continued to wait for an agent to become free, the baggage handlers got into what appeared to be verbal fisticuffs imploring the agents to hurry up. It quickly became obvious that one of the agents was getting frustrated with all of the bantering. When he finished processing the passengers ahead of us, he quickly turned away in a huff and left the check-in counter. In a few minutes he returned with another gentleman who I assumed was his supervisor. He then confronted the baggage handlers. After what appeared to be a rather short terse conversation with them, the three men handed over their ID badges and were quickly escorted away.

One can only imagine what might have happened to them. I was glad I wasn't in their shoes. Momentarily, another baggage handler was instructed to assist us and he started off where the others began — by once again asking our group for tips. At that point he really didn't have anything left to do for us. Our sponsor who was traveling with us tried to explain as best as he could that we had already given our tips to the other baggage handlers and in essence we had nothing left to give him. After a few minutes of insisting he finally quit asking and we were able to get our bags checked through to be placed on the plane. Our group then headed upstairs to the boarding area. Next stop — Erbil Iraq! After another short wait and one final security check the team headed over to a passenger lounge area to await the boarding process.

A short time later we were escorted out of the terminal and onto the tarmac where we walked toward an all-white, virtually unmarked 737 jet. The only distinct marking was the name "Jessica." Everyone found that to be a little odd, but we headed up the stairs to find our assigned seats.

Once airborne the flight was uneventful, and two hours later we landed at Erbil International Airport. The plane taxied to the terminal area and as the doors of the aircraft opened, we each took our first breath of unfiltered air in Iraq. We quickly descended down the mobile stairs and in essence into a war zone that would be our home for the next several days.

I stood momentarily at the bottom of the stairs soaking in our surroundings. I noticed that the airport was fairly small with just a few outer buildings. As everyone gathered below on the tarmac we were met by a small contingent of Kurdish officials. I recognized one of them from a luncheon I had attended some months back in San Francisco.

A few of us started to take some pictures, but were quickly asked not to due to security reasons. With a show of disappointment we stowed our cameras for the moment. Over the next several days we would have ample opportunity to take pictures and video of the areas we were scheduled to visit.

After a round of introductions we were ushered into a separate building away from the other passengers where a security person asked us to surrender our passports. One of our hosts then led us over to a sitting area where we were served a traditional tea — sweet and very tasty. Soon the security person reappeared to return our passports to us. We were now cleared to step outside to get some fresh air and once again take in our surroundings. For the first time my presence in the war-torn country of Iraq completely soaked in. This was the place where our son Matthew had laid down his life for his fellow man. After a few moments I was asked to go back inside and our group was led through another exit where a small Mercedes bus waited to transport us to our hotel. We were escorted by three unmarked security vehicles. It was apparent that our little convoy was transporting a group of very important people.

As the sun began to set, our driver maneuvered his way through the streets of Erbil. There were cars everywhere — going every which way. A thought crossed my mind as we traveled along the road. Perhaps somebody had forgotten to tell the citizens of Erbil that there was a war going on in their own backyard. Our driver and the escorts in front and behind us were able to force their way in and out of traffic with ease. The local people recognized this as a government convoy of sorts and would move or yield as necessary to allow our caravan to pass.

We arrived at the hotel where we recognized the distinct protection of a bomb blast wall surrounding the area. As we approached the wall we saw a mural through the entrance that reflected a peaceful scene of flowers and children at play. The mural expressed the freedom the Iraqis now enjoyed since Saddam no longer lived to terrorize them. This northern region of Iraq where Erbil was located was somewhat protected by the no-fly zone established after the first Gulf War of the early 1990s.

At the end of the wall the bus made a sharp right turn into the entrance that was well protected by armed Soldiers stationed at a gatepost. The gate was lifted for our bus and escort vehicles, and we drove up to the hotel entrance. As we gazed at the hotel ahead of us I thought how modern and beautiful it appeared. Everyone disembarked, and as with our hotel in Amman, we were required to pass through metal detectors to enter. We were asked to surrender any weapons before entering the safety of the lobby. If anyone had a gun it was placed in a drawer. As I passed through I glanced over and noticed there were quite a few pistols in it. Just another reminder of the region we were visiting. The interior of the hotel was equally adorned as the outside, and just as beautiful.

We quickly checked in and received our room keys before being led to a dining area to await the arrival of what in the days to come would be many dignitaries and officials of the Kurdish government of Northern Iraq. That evening we were to meet the Kurdish Minister of Foreign Relations. After a short wait the Minister arrived and formally extended his welcome on behalf of the government and citizens of Kurdistan. The words and expressions that followed were in many ways healing and honoring. He started by acknowledging the loss of our sons in helping the people of Iraq to be free from Saddam Hussein. He went on to explain that religious freedom was a priority for Kurdistan, because it was essential to their overall and longstanding freedom.

I listened in amazement to what was being said, and a sense of great comfort came over me. I gleaned a better understanding for why our boys are willing to give their lives for our country. If the Minister's words were any indication, their sacrifice would forever be remembered by a grateful people. It reaffirmed to me that American lives had been given to do the right thing — to help the nation of Iraq.

Each of us took the time to thank the Minister for his kind words, after which we sat down for dinner. Given that I was still feeling a little under the weather and in a weakened state, I ate very little food. After the dinner had concluded, I said goodnight to the group and headed up to my room.

Probably the most important thing I needed at that point was a good night's rest. I estimated I had been up for about thirty-six hours. It was time to sleep and get well rested for the days ahead.

The Sentencing

John:

The next morning I felt more rested, and although somewhat still weak, began to prepare for my first full day in Iraq. I looked at the date on my watch and it showed November 6, 2006. Almost one year had passed since Matthew and the others on his patrol were killed.

I turned on the TV to the BBC announcing the news that Saddam Hussein had been sentenced to death by hanging. Scenes of the Shia Muslims celebrating in the streets interrupted those of Sunni Muslims expressing outrage. The announcer said the Iranians thought the sentencing was just, and the United States called it a great day for the Iraqi people. Amnesty International stated that the trial was "Unfair — completely unfair!" As I heard this latter comment I thought, *Was Saddam fair*? *Hello*? What planet were these people living on, anyway? Had they not seen the atrocities he had brought upon his own nation? As I continued to watch this news being played on the worldwide stage, I knew this was an historical moment. How ironic that I was in Iraq on this very day to witness this news event.

At first I thought how the man that could have been one of Iraq's greatest leaders squandered the opportunity to help his people by becoming a tyrant. Ultimately, he would get his just do. And, then a strange feeling came over me as I watched him portrayed on television. I began to feel sorry for the man who was responsible for so many deaths, including Mathew's. I believed he deserved his sentence many times over — you reap what you sow. But at that moment I felt sorry for him. His life could have been so much different and the lives of the people of Iraq could have been different as well. I was still in the grip of my own grief-wracked soul, and yet I sat in this hotel room in a country that Saddam had nearly destroyed, I was overcome with an absolute feeling of compassion. I will never understand why those entrusted to lead others choose to become dictators or bullies who think they'll get away with murdering, maiming and destroying the very fabric of the nation they were given the responsibility of leading. How sad!

Downstairs I joined the group for breakfast — another buffet spread. This time I chose the blandest items I could find like flat bread and humus mixed with some scrambled eggs. My appetite had still not returned, but as a diabetic I needed something to sustain my energy for the rest of the day.

As we finished our meal we learned that our first visit of the day would take us to the city center known as the Citadel. Our host explained that the Citadel was the oldest continuously occupied city on earth. Later in the day we were scheduled to meet with President Barzani's Chief of Staff.

We proceeded outside to board our minibus and headed out of the heavily guarded compound of our hotel escorted by two security vehicles. One vehicle drove ahead of us, while the other followed behind onto the streets of Erbil. As we reached the main road, I noticed a number of armed Soldiers lining the streets. The Soldiers stood about every 100 feet along the roadside, AK-47s in hand.

Our escorts told us they had been called on to quell any unrest because of the Saddam verdict. However, I believed the Soldiers were there to waylay any excessive celebration by the Kurdish people. After all, hadn't Saddam tried to wipe them off the face of the earth?

We drove through the streets of Erbil until we came to the base of a hill surrounded by an old wall. The drivers followed the wall around until they came to an opening where two armed Soldiers stood guard at the entrance to the Citadel. The Soldiers waved our vehicles through, and we began to climb a dirt road to the upper level where the drivers parked. Through the window I caught a glimpse of what appeared to be an ancient mud/brick wall. We disembarked and were led on a tour of the surrounding buildings.

The tour was fantastic. The scenery looked like something one would envision from Biblical times. Our guide shared that it was the hope of the Kurdish people to refurbish the structure and turn it into a tourist destination. To accomplish the wishes of the people, The State Organization of Antiquities and Heritage had undertaken an ambitious program to restore and develop the Qalah. As we continued walking I noticed a sign mounted on a wall that stated the following:

Qalah of Erbil

"Erbil is the oldest city constantly inhabited. The Qalah consists of 3 quarters, Takiya, Topkhana and Saray. The Qalah has witnessed all epochs of Mesopotamian history and pre-history from

1000 B.C. until the Present. It has been for some time the religious centre of the Assyrians. The goddess Ishtar was the paramount goddess of the city. Sennachrib the great king of Assyria — (705 B.C. - 681 B.C.), supplied the Qalah with water through a very sophisticated system of aqueducts deriving from Bastora 22km to the north. The name Orbelym was derived from Sumerian text."

As we toured the area we saw a few shops and museums on the site, but there was still much work to be done to restore and improve the area for future tourists. Our guide led us through several buildings and eventually up a stairway to the roof where we were able to get a 360-degree view of the city.

As was the custom during Biblical times people chose sites like this Citadel on high ground for security purposes. From this vantage point the enemy could be seen approaching from any direction, giving the residents a strategic advantage.

The view was incredible. We could see people going about their daily lives down below and cars mixed with animal-drawn carts. Tall buildings were being constructed among the ancient and smaller buildings with the use of even taller cranes. It was clear that Erbil was a city in transition — a city reflecting the hope of a nation that had been given a new chance. I noticed TV antennas and satellite dishes on rooftops, even on the Citadel itself. I watched three small children playing in a courtyard, and occasionally I saw someone walking in the distance between buildings. There were people still living among the ancient buildings of this impressive fortress. We watched in awe and took pictures until our guides said it was time to go to our next location on the other side of the Citadel known as the Rug Museum.

The Rug Museum was a collection of rugs, furniture, cooking implements and other household items from days long gone. It was an interesting assortment of items, and the rugs were very colorful.

As we toured the various areas throughout that day, we were always aware that in our shadow a well-dressed security detail kept close watch over us. Knowing this allowed us to relax enough to be able to contemplate the seriousness of why we had come to Iraq, that amongst other things we were there to observe and write down our stories. We wanted to take in our surroundings so when we returned to the United States we could share the truth of the good things our young men and women were doing to help a nation rebuild.

Our Citadel tour came to an end, and we boarded the bus for our return to the hotel to eat and rest before our afternoon schedule. Upon arriving we encountered a foreign film crew documenting a story on the women of Kurdistan. They were curious about our presence and after learning a little about our story, asked if they could interview us.

For the next thirty minutes we talked about our sons, the purpose of our visit, our observations to that point, and what we hoped to achieve on the remainder of our trip. After the interview concluded, we thanked the film crew and grabbed a quick bite

We were then escorted to another area of the hotel to meet the Chief of Staff. He expressed the appreciation of the Kurdish people for the sacrifices our children had made, conveying that he recognized that our loss was different than their own because they were fighting for their freedom and America had come to help them achieve that freedom. He went on to say, "This war is a different kind of war, where you fight first and then both sides sit down and talk. In this war we will win or they will win. They are the enemies of the civilized world."

After the Chief of Staff departed we resumed our tour. We were driven out of town on what seemed like a Sunday afternoon drive. The driver took us from the relatively flat area around Erbil into a more mountainous area with trees and a small river that led to a beautiful countryside.

John surrounded by Iraqi children during his visit in November 2006.

We were headed to the town of Shaqlawa. Our driver told us that Shaqlawa was a resort town where the Iraqis escaped the summer heat in the coolness of the mountains. We arrived at our destination in the late afternoon. Shadowed by our security team we were allowed to stroll down the streets while visiting with the local people and browsing through the shops. The shops sold fruit, candies, nuts, trinkets and all manner of things. Our hosts pointed out some of their favorite treats.

A small cluster of children who were curious about us surrounded our group. It was great to see their smiling faces. I was reminded of the same smiles captured in a photo we had received of Matthew in Taji just days before his death. One of my personal desires on this trip was to get a similar picture of myself with the children so I could experience Matthew's feelings when the kids surrounded him.

I asked one of the others to indulge me and take a picture. One click and my mission was accomplished.

It started raining while we were in Shaqlawa, and I noticed a drop in temperature. Our guides led us over to a local teahouse, and for the next hour we sat around discussing the events of the day and enjoying our nice hot cups of tea. For the first time since our trip began, I felt relaxed. It must have been a combination of the cool air, the warm tea and new friends. It was a great memory under otherwise sad circumstances.

Soon it was time to head back to our hotel. We boarded the bus and in a short period were back on the main road to Erbil. Our ride was uneventful, and within a short period of time we were passing through the blast walls and by the armed guards, once again through the metal detectors and into the safety of the hotel.

That evening after dinner the group made our way to the lounge area to unwind and talk about the events of our day. Later in the privacy of my room I made a note. I believe it sums up that first full day in Iraq perfectly. I wrote: *Matthew will forever be a part of the country of Iraq by virtue of his blood that was spilled and soaked into the soil of Taji, and as his Father I am here to honor him.*

A Grateful People

_____

John:

It's been six days since we began our journey, and to this point I'd experienced everything I'd expected and much more. Based on a discussion with our guide the night before, I knew we would be visiting a number of high profile areas in contrast to the tourist locations of the previous day.

The gentlemen traveling in the group were asked to wear our coats and ties that we had brought with us. At breakfast we learned more about our itinerary for the day. Our first stop would be a visit with the U.S. Army troops stationed at Camp Zaytun, a South Korean Army base in the area. We learned that about 200 U.S. troops were stationed there, and we were excited to be getting an opportunity to visit with them.

Breakfast wrapped up and we headed out to board our bus. By now all of us were familiar with the bus routine — cruising at high speeds whenever possible to avoid trouble, weaving in and out of traffic and followed closely by our escort vehicles in the front and rear of our caravan.

Camp Zaytun was located near the airport where we had landed. The main function of the camp was to provide aid in the reconstruction effort in Iraq. Those stationed there advised the Iraqis in areas of economic development as well as educational and medical services programs. A key approach in partnering with the Iraqis in the region was through vocational training that the multi-national Soldiers provided to the local residents.

Within the hour we arrived outside Camp Zaytun. As we approached the front gate Korean Soldiers in full combat gear quickly waved us through security. Once inside I saw quite a few large earthen berms in place of the blast walls we had seen on the streets of Erbil and at our hotel. In addition, there were strategically placed heavy pieces of weaponry hidden under camouflage netting.

We drove around to the U.S. Army section of the base and immediately in sight were three Humvees. As I looked at them a feeling of sadness came over me, as images flashed through my mind of the photos of

101

Matthew's Humvee. Within a split second I was re-living the events of November 2005 all over again. The ring of the doorbell, the notification, and what little details were provided to Stacey and me in terms of what actually happened the day Matt died. It's probably understandable that the sight of a Humvee amongst other things would be a trigger for me — split second flashes of memories that took me back to a place in my mind where I preferred not to go. It's like your brain is loaded with images, some real, some imagined and when you encounter something or someone those images are triggered in rapid fashion. Those who have experienced a traumatic event such as the death of a loved one, more so your only child, know those feelings are not pleasant to encounter. I understood I wasn't going to make it through this trip without having at least one such episode.

Our driver came to a stop near the dining facility known as the DFAC where we were to meet the U.S. Army officer in charge and some of the Soldiers stationed at the camp. The next hour or so proved to be quite emotional for all of us, especially the parents. We introduced ourselves and recounted our son's stories and those of their brothers in arms.

As I shared Matthew's story, I told them that we were behind them one hundred and ten percent. I was honored to be standing in Iraq with American Soldiers and having the opportunity to personally thank them from the bottom of my heart for a job well done. I expressed that their work to help reconstruct Iraq was honorable and right. And, that as tough as it might be to lose one of their own, they could stand on knowing that he or she lost their life protecting and serving an honorable and just cause. By this point the tears began to flow. As was often the case over those first months, I choked up. Tears came far too easily for me since November 16, 2005.

As all Gold Star parents Stacey and I were collateral damage. We might as well have been in that Humvee with Matthew when the IED went off. Both of us were deeply wounded by the loss of our son and only child. In those early days and months it was so difficult to contain our emotions — to try to make sense of any of it. This trip to Iraq was part of my effort to heal and figure out a way that we could recover. After spending time sharing from our hearts, we were served coffee and given the opportunity to chat with the Soldiers one-on-one. One young man told me that he was from San Diego. In fact he lived just a short distance from our home.

A moment later everyone made their way outside to take some pictures before we headed to our next destination. I took a few minutes to make my way over to the area where a few of the Humvees were parked. This is the closest I'd been to one in the past year. I made my way around to the right-side rear passenger door and gazed inside. That is where Matthew would have been sitting on that dreadful day just one year prior. I could envision seeing him sitting there in that seat. Why hadn't the up-armored protection saved him on that fateful day? All I could do was shake my head and walk away.

Everyone gathered around to take a final picture while the parents held a banner showing our support for those wonderful young men and women serving our nation 10,000 miles from the comforts of home. We said our goodbyes and shook hands with the Soldiers, thanking them for taking the time to meet with us. As we left Camp Kaytun, I glanced back for one last look at the Humvees and snapped a few more pictures of the Korean Soldiers and the artillery equipment.

We passed through the security gate and onto the main road heading for our next meeting which would be with the Kurdish President Mahmoud Barzani.

After a short drive we arrived at the presidential residence located in the countryside near Erbil. We were invited inside and led into a large, ornately decorated sitting room. President Barzani was awaiting our arrival, and once we entered he took his designated seat at the head of the room. He was dressed in traditional Kurdish clothing and wore a red checked head scarf known as a Keffiyeh.

As we were served traditional tea, President Barzani very eloquently expressed his condolences for the loss of our sons. At the same time he was quick to remind us that the Kurdish region of Iraq had also suffered the loss of many lives in their cause for freedom. The meeting was very pleasant, and after thirty minutes the President stood to leave. Our meeting concluded, we exited the residence and posed for pictures on the front steps before getting back on the bus.

The next stop was the residence of Prime Minister Nechirvan Barzani. We were invited inside and seated in an even larger lavishly decorated room with a setup similar to that at the presidential residence. Once again we were served tea, and then a well-dressed Prime Minister walked in and took his seat at the head of the room. I noticed the striking difference between the older President Barzani in his traditional clothing and the younger Prime Minister in his nicely tailored suit and tie. It truly reflected the contrast between what had been and what will be — a younger generation of Iraqis and Kurds looking to the future that would hopefully be better than their past. At that moment the simple word FREEDOM came to my mind. After about thirty minutes of conversation with the Prime Minister, we finished our tea and again headed outside to take a few pictures on the front steps of the ministry building. We concluded our visit by thanking the Prime Minister for meeting with us and once again climbed aboard our bus to head to our next destination.

After a short distance our driver maneuvered our vehicle through a set of gates to a former Iraqi Army base that had been turned into a memorial park. He slowly made his way over to a large stone patio area with fountains and a large dark stone memorial approximately 25 feet high. As we approached the structure we noticed names inscribed on the stone in both Kurdish and English. The names reflected the Kurds that had been killed in a suicide bomb attack in February 2004. On that day close to a hundred citizens lost their lives, including family members of our hosts and guides for this trip.

The Iraqi media was also at this location to cover the visit of the American Gold Star parents. For the next hour the group indulged them while pictures and videos were taken of our visit to the Memorial. The footage would be shown later that evening on the local stations in Erbil. Once the formal media event concluded we spent some time alone walking around the area taking pictures and observing the different sights. Afterwards, we boarded our bus for a short drive over to a restaurant in the park where we were treated to a very nice meal on behalf of our hosts. We spent the next couple of hours until just before sunset relaxing and recalling the events up to that point in our day.

Before the day ended we would have one more meeting. We met with a filmmaker who was doing a documentary in an effort to raise awareness about the Kurdish people. The documentary was about the men who had been abducted and driven into the desert and executed, never to be seen again. That was until the filmmaker made it his mission to try and find them.

He told us Saddam Hussein had killed nearly 300,000 Iraqi citizens in this fashion. He showed us a documentary film about his journey to an area south of Kurdistan where some of those unfortunate people were buried. The good news was he had successfully located some of the remains. The bad news was that without the proper DNA technology it would be nearly impossible to identify them. He hoped that we would be able to help him.

It was evident that this gentleman was very courageous in what he was trying to do, especially given the danger that still existed in the region. Some of the footage showed him and others armed to the teeth as they traveled into hostile territory to uncover the lost souls that Saddam and those who had supported him hoped would never be found. I pray that he was successful in securing the funds and support he needed to help the families of the Iraqi's fallen locate the remains of their loved ones.

Darkness had fallen and we were feeling the effects of a very long day. Before we headed back to the hotel we stopped for one final visit at the home of one of the hosts of our trip. As the bus traveled down the dark the road it was impossible to tell where we were. Yet as we approached the home I could tell by the reflection off the bus's headlights that it was fairly nice from the outside.

We disembarked and were invited into the home where we were introduced to the mother of one of our sponsors. She conveyed her pleasure at our visit, and expressed her condolences to the group. Our sponsor had previously told us that the memorial park we had visited earlier in the day was dedicated to her father and brother who were both killed in the suicide blast. But we also learned she had established a foundation to provide for the less fortunate children of Kurdistan. As a group we expressed our willingness to help if able. At this point it was fairly late in the evening and as the meeting wrapped up, we bid farewell and boarded the bus for our ride back to the hotel.

What a day! I'd never thought I would do the unusual things we did that day. I would trade all of it to go back to our normal life and to have our son back again.

Anfal

John:

After a restful night I met up with everyone to grab some breakfast and discuss our itinerary for the day. In many ways our schedule would be similar to the day before. More meetings with dignitaries and more opportunities for the Kurdish leadership to tell their story to us so we could take it back to the American people.

Our first visit of the day would be with the Minister of the Interior. Unlike the day before, the building we were ushered into was surrounded by a large concrete blast wall with armed Soldiers at the front security gate. Our vehicle was quickly waved through the gate. We were led up a sweeping staircase to the third floor and into yet another meeting room. This room was equally ornate with red velvet furniture. We settled into our seats for the traditional tea while exchanging greetings with the Minister. He conveyed his condolences for our son's sacrifices and went on to express his sincere gratitude to the United States for helping Iraq escape tyranny.

The conversation followed a similar theme to our previous meetings with one exception. As an added bonus we learned that in the room next door to where we were meeting with the Minister, there were a handful of U.S. Army officers visiting from Afghanistan. The Minister asked if we would like to meet them to which we all replied a resounding, Yes! A few minutes later they entered the room and we exchanged hugs and handshakes, along with our grateful thanks for their service. Clearly that moment was another highlight of our visit. All too soon it was time to go and say our goodbyes. We headed out of the meeting room and as we descended the grand staircase we took the opportunity to take a few more pictures. Then we extended our thanks to the Minister and boarded the bus to our next destination.

Our next meeting was with the Minister of the Anfal Martyrs. In the span of a few minutes we arrived at the entrance to a building that

107

reminded me of a typical government building — very utilitarian. Once inside we were led into a small room very different from the ornate rooms we had met in over the past few days. Shortly after we sat down, the Minister joined us to offer her insights about the Anfal Campaign.

She was a petite woman who appeared to be in her mid-thirties. After greeting us she began explaining the purpose of her office. She said that immediately following our meeting we would be taken to a village outside of Erbil to see for ourselves what the tyranny of Saddam Hussein's rule had done to his own countrymen. She explained that "Al-Anfal" was the term they used to describe the genocide that Saddam Hussein had perpetrated on the Iraqi people in the northern Kurdish region. His purpose was to either drive the Kurds completely out of Iraq all together — or to exterminate them — much as Hitler did to the Jewish people.

During the Anfal Campaign Saddam's army destroyed thousands of small villages and moved the inhabitants into crudely built concentration camps with open sewers and no running water or electricity. He commanded the military to round up the Kurdish people in an effort to completely control every aspect of their livelihood. That way the Iraq government could easily do as they pleased with them. That was not unlike what the Jews encountered in Poland when they were trapped in the Warsaw Ghettos.

The Minister went on to state that by controlling the population in a segregated area whenever an Iraqi official wanted, they could simply round up family members — primarily the men — and take them away from their homes never to be seen or heard from again. Their families could only assume they had been murdered. As a result, there was a detrimental societal impact to the Kurdish culture. According to their customs, if a married woman's husband left their home, she could not re-marry if the husband or his body could not be found. Since the Iraqi military had no intention of returning the husband's body, his wife would not be able to remarry, nor have more children. Thus, if the women could no longer bear children, there would no longer be a Kurdish population.

All I could think as I was listening to the Minister was *how diabolical*! *How much hate could one person have*?

After the Minister was done with her presentation it was time for our group to travel to one of the villages to meet some of the survivors of Saddam's atrocities. By the time we headed out it was late afternoon. As we left the Ministry it became apparent that our convoy had grown. Our normal security detail mentioned that the Minister was worried about our safety and that our well-being was of utmost concern. By all toll I counted eight vehicles in our convoy instead of our usual three. In addition, there were a number of Soldiers assigned to our detail whose sole responsibility was to block the roads ahead of our procession. It was quite the ride, high speed and bumpy as we turned off the main road.

As we approached the village, I couldn't help but notice the change in landscape. It was rocky, devoid of any foliage and barren. I saw some kids off in the distance playing soccer in the dirt, and then I noticed a person on a motorcycle coming out of the field. What occurred over the next several minutes was enough to make anyone nervous.

As I continued watching it seemed as if the motorcyclist was on a direct course for our bus, and the driver had caught my complete attention. The motorcycle looked fairly new, red in color, and had a small trunk on the back of the seat. The driver appeared to be a young man. At that point our convoy had slowed for some reason and while we were still moving forward it seemed as if the motorcyclist kept adjusting his course in a straight line toward our bus.

From everything I'd heard prior to traveling to the Middle East, this seemed like a text book scenario for a suicide bomber. Finally, the moment of truth. The motorcyclist came within about thirty feet of our bus and I thought, *was this to be our demise*? This is what had happened so many times to our troops, to the sailors of the USS Cole and even as we had learned just the day before to innocent bystanders in the countries throughout the region. At that exact point there was nothing I could do other than to convince myself that my worry was for naught. And then he was there, through the window I gauged him to be no more than ten feet away from our bus when he suddenly veered off and zoomed past us. What a relief!

A few minutes later we made our way into the village, and as the driver parked our vehicle we experienced our first sight of the dwellings that were very poorly constructed with concrete block. The dwellings were attached one to another in long rows with narrow streets of dirt in between that served more as alleys. It quickly became apparent that we were clearly amongst the poorest people of Erbil.

As we stepped down from our bus, we were led over to a couple of different homes where the residents, through interpreters, told stories of their family's losses. Some explained accounts of losing many, if not all of their family members. One woman we met related how both of her sons were taken from their home never to be seen again, and with tears in her eyes she brought out pictures to show us. Even though it had been many years since they were taken away, she still cried for them. It was easy to understand exactly how she felt.

Another woman we met was the sole survivor of her entire family. All toll she had lost twenty three-family members. I couldn't help but be overcome with sadness and shed tears at her loss. These were things most of us had learned from the past in our history books, not something one could fathom would still be occurring in this modern era.

As we exited the alley, I noticed a small crowd of children standing nearby watching and listening to everything that was being said. I decided to approach and take some video of them. They quickly surrounded me, hamming it up and jostling with each other. They clearly enjoyed being filmed, and as I captured them on video I flipped the camcorder screen around to let them see themselves being filmed. What hit my heart at that very moment was this is what childhood was meant to be — *Carefree* — *Worry free*!

As I think back on that scene, I can't help but smile at the memories we'd built in the minds of those kids that day. As much as any of the rest of our trips would convey, for me the visit to the village that day reaffirmed that America was in Iraq for the right reasons. That more than a fight for oil, or religious rights, this was a fight for humanity. Throughout our visit the officials we had met consistently told us how much they appreciated the United States for taking a stand to help their nation. That moment amongst those children confirmed that truth.

As I'd stood there filming I recalled a time when someone said that when you visit a person's home you can tell how the adults really feel about you by how their children react to you. If the adults love and appreciate you, the children will reflect those same emotions — but, if the adults showed no outward signs of affection, then their children would in turn reflect the same. The fact that those children were eager to be friendly with the Americans was a confirmation that they had been told we were a good and just people. As I looked into the children's eyes I could see the future generation of Iraq, and there was no doubt in my mind that they were worth saving.

Daylight was beginning to fade and our security detail informed us that we needed to leave the area. As I packed up my camera gear I stopped momentarily to have another parent take a few still pictures of me with the children before we loaded up on the bus. Those pictures have become a treasure for me. I often find myself reflecting back on them with the honor of being given the opportunity to make this trip and to personally hear the stories from those closest to the real world experience.

*   *   *

Our final meeting that day would be with the Minister of Finance in his home. In contrast to the squalor of the village we had just visited, his residence was nicely decorated, very ornate and themed in blue. In my opinion that was one of the best meetings, although each meeting was good in its own right. It started with the Minister telling us that he was a Christian. Of course, my first thought was how awesome it was that there was a Christian as a key official in a predominately Muslim government. It was truly a blessing to hear this. He told us how Saddam's Baathist regime had destroyed over 3500 Christian churches in the Kurdish region by any means available to the Iraqi Army. Iraq's Christian population had at one time numbered over one million people; a population that had existed in the region several thousand years before the spread of Islam in 600 A.D.

No wonder that many of the structures destroyed were of ancient historical value. According to Biblical records, the prophet Jonah preached repentance to the inhabitants of the Assyrian city of Nineveh near the modern city of Mosul 700 years before the birth of Christ. In the years leading up to our visit many thousands of Christians had fled Iraq to neighboring countries — to as far away as Europe and the United States — all to avoid religious persecution, otherwise known as ethnic cleansing. I recall hearing in the media how some of those displaced citizens had even made their way to San Diego.

As the Minister continued, he mentioned that the Kurdish government was committed to rebuilding the churches and in fact they were assisting Christians who wanted to relocate back to the region. That last statement caught me by surprise, so much so that I felt compelled to interrupt him. I repeated what he had said about financially assisting Christians to relocate. He reaffirmed that was exactly what he'd said, which completely blew me away.

He went on to show us information packages that the government had put together to encourage the return of the Iraqi Christians. To be honest, I thought I was dreaming. Not only were the words a blessing to hear, but absolutely amazing as well. It was encouraging to hear that Kurdish citizens who had fled Iraq were being persuaded to return and to unite with their countrymen and family members, not based on being divided by religious lines, but based on a common desire to rebuild their nation.

The Kurds may not be a perfect people, but I think anyone would agree that based on what we had learned, credit needed to be given where credit was due. Our visit with the Minister came to a conclusion, and as we gathered our belongings he again graciously extended his thanks to us for traveling all the way to Iraq to learn for ourselves the real story. As we parted he gave us each a small gift for our visit and we thanked him for his hospitality and said our goodbyes.

Within the hour we arrived back at the hotel. I had previously learned that very early the next morning I would be calling into the Roger Hedgecock radio show back in San Diego. Since it was fairly late, and San Diego was a ten hour time difference behind Iraq, I decided it was probably best to head straight to my room to get a couple of hours of sleep so I could sound somewhat coherent for the audience.

Of course as luck would have it, and even though I was pretty tired, I still woke up way before I needed too. Rather than risk missing my call-in time, I decided to stay awake and jot down some notes reflecting back on the events of the past couple of days. Finally, it was time for me to call in for my slot on the radio show. The producer who answered my call passed me directly through to Roger.

Over the past year I had called into Roger's show a number of times to discuss the various aspects of the legislative work Stacey and I were doing on The Holley Provision. As with those previous calls Roger was very complimentary and after a brief introduction, he allowed me to share Matthew's story with the audience and asked me to highlight the reason for my trip to Iraq. There was no doubt that the past few days had filled my heart and mind with many things to share. The most important message I hoped to convey to the listeners was that as an American Gold Star parent, I along with the other mothers and fathers had been given an opportunity to witness with our own eyes why our children had given the ultimate sacrifice.

If I took anything anyway from this journey, it was resting in knowing Matthew did not die in vain. Rather, our sons gave their lives for a noble and just cause — the cause of freedom from oppression! That because of their sacrifices a foundation had been laid for the Iraqi people to begin helping themselves and healing their nation. That our sons, and for that matter all of our servicemen and women, had helped the Iraqi people accomplish great things since they had been freed from Saddam's tyrannical rule.

My interview lasted about twenty minutes and ended with Roger thanking me for calling in at what he knew was a very early morning hour in Iraq. I again expressed my thanks to him for allowing me to tell the story of a grateful nation — a story not being told in the mainstream media at that time. A story that the Iraqis we spoke to hoped we would share. I could now say I had taken the first of many steps to do just that. Each day of that trip had clearly been filled with eye-opening events that unmasked the veil of a hurting nation — a nation learning to live and bask in the glory of its newfound freedom. I was certain there was more to learn. Still early when the call concluded I decided to take a nap before the day's activities kicked into high gear.

The Red House

<u>John</u>:

Day eight of our journey took us on a long road trip to the town of Sulaymaniyah near the Iranian border, home to one of Saddam Hussein's most dreaded prisons known as the "Red House." To the Kurdish people it was an unforgiving place where citizens were taken in the middle of the night and tortured by the Iraqi military — some never to be seen again. I remember that as one of the most emotionally moving days of the entire trip.

Our morning began with our usual breakfast, small talk and boarding the bus. I noticed that our security detail was more heavily armed than in days past. It wasn't unusual that those seeking to cause problems from the Iranian side would cross over and cause havoc in the Iraqi border towns. So for this trip we would have to live with AK-47s stored in the front cab of the bus near our security team. The sight of more weapons reminded me of the extreme danger to travelers in this part of the world. Our group members did not have the luxury of wearing body armor for protection that one typically saw American civilians wearing while traveling throughout Iraq. I believe it was an unspoken rule that before any of us ever said yes to traveling to Iraq, we'd placed our fate completely in God's hands.

We made our way through the streets of Erbil until we reached the open road. Once there our driver quickly accelerated to a high rate of speed. In front of us was another vehicle with several security personnel inside. The lead vehicle was now far ahead of us, and we were passing everyone in sight to keep within range. As we sped along I noticed the sights and landmarks of the countryside. There were a number of Army outposts and rural homes. A vast majority of the structures were small and made of stone. I saw acre upon acre of newly planted trees.

One of the gentlemen escorting us told me that it was part of a re-forestation program that the government had put in place. He went on to explain that during the war, part of Saddam Hussein's plan for killing off the Kurdish population was to deprive them of any food, shelter or other basic necessities of life. Since the trees were a source of fuel and heat for the Kurds, Saddam had them systematically destroyed by chemical means. What he couldn't kill by poison he set on fire. In the end, the remaining few trees were cut down by the Kurds and used for fuel or heat.

Now during the relative calm of a newly found freedom the people had been given the opportunity to be part of the reforestation effort for the northern region of Iraq. After traveling for over an hour we stopped for our first break at a private home in a small town. The countryside surrounding the town was very beautiful, and our hosts were so gracious, supplying us with water and allowing us to stretch our legs and use the restroom before heading on toward Sulaymaniyah.

Our next stop was the larger town of Quoia. After parking the vehicle we took a walking tour of the nearby sights. People were out on the sidewalks and not surprisingly all eyes were on us. I enjoyed the atmosphere of the town as it reminded me of something from days of old. Most of us had our cameras readily available, and we snapped lots of pictures. I took one of a lone donkey standing in a vacant lot and one of my favorite sights, the old Soviet era farm tractors driving down the middle of the street. As we continued our walk I noticed an older man dressed in traditional Kurdish clothing. I showed him my camera and pointed to him and then to the camera to ask if I could take his picture. A big smile immediately lit up his face, and he stood up as if at attention to pose for me. It was great to see his face when I showed him the image on the digital screen. He had the biggest smile anyone could imagine. As I walked away I gave him a thumbs-up and he gave me one back. It was very heartwarming to find no hate in his eyes — only respect and friendship.

The market area and shops we visited were right out of the History Channel. They displayed fruits, vegetables and crudely butchered meat hanging on hooks. We went through an old bazaar where other items were sold such as clothing, accessories and jewelry. I loved that little town and the simple life it reflected. What a contrast to the way so many live in the United States.

As we continued our walk I saw a gentleman across from us wearing traditional clothes with a pistol tucked in the sash around his waist. I don't remember a smile from him, only a stare. As I look back I wonder if it was a stare of anger or curiosity. I suppose I'll never really know. Soon our walking tour was over. We returned to the bus and headed out of town to ascend some very high mountains. In anticipation of a wild ride I broke out my video camera to record that portion of our journey.

We began climbing the mountains at a fairly normal pace, but that didn't last long. Soon we were speeding our way up a winding mountain road. It felt like we were on a roller coaster ride, except there was no downhill for a long time. We went back and forth and back and forth, and the higher we went the steeper the cliffs became. The views were spectacular for as far as the eye could see. Up and up we went until we finally reached the top.

Our driver pulled over to the side of the road where there were two abandoned military observation posts, and we were allowed to get out of the bus to stretch our legs and check them out. The view of the hillside and mountains from that vantage point was absolutely breathtaking. We took note as our hosts pointed off to the east, explaining that the mountains in the distance were those of the Iranian high plains. We were close — almost too close for comfort! There was a reason those observation posts were located where they were. From that vantage point the Iraqi's kept watch over their border against the potential of an invasion from Iran.

After about fifteen minutes we took off for the steep and winding descent to the valley below. As we descended into the foothills the scenery reminded me of the back roads of San Diego County, scrub brush and desert. We made our way out of the foothills and into the wide flat valley below. Once again the driver picked up speed and began passing everything in sight.

At one of the earlier stops during our trip I'd mentioned to our host that the driver seemed to have no fear of passing vehicles on hills or in blind curves. I thought that was completely insane. Our host assured me that our safety was at the forefront of his mind. He explained that the lead vehicle was in communication with the security person driving our vehicle. The lead vehicle would radio back to our driver and tell them it was okay to pass even though as passengers we couldn't see that for ourselves. His explanation still did not reassure me one hundred percent, but I had to trust that they knew what they were doing, and that their training was adequate to ensure our safety. My faith was clearly in full force for the rest of the trip that day. I made an attempt to ignore my concerns, relax and enjoy our journey.

We turned onto what appeared to be a newly constructed highway, another example of investment being poured into the infrastructure of the region. Our guides pointed out a recently enhanced electrical grid for the area as well as a cement plant off in the distance. I couldn't tell if the plant was releasing smoke or dust, but it was clear it was going full bore.

Clearly these were symbols of the progress the Kurdish people were making in rebuilding their towns and cities. A new cement plant reflected a vital investment toward success of the construction going on in the region. This was yet another mixture of old and new literally side by side. We also passed what appeared to be an ancient fortress and were told it was currently being used as a prison. It was clear how useful it was as a prison, given that solid stone had been used to build the ancient structure.

After about an hour's drive we were near the outskirts of Sulaymaniyah when our guide recited a story about a famous restaurant in town called "MaDonals." No, not McDonald's, MaDonals. He went on to say that the real McDonald's Corporation had been in contact with the owner of MaDonals to cease using that name and any other similarities, such as the famous golden arches.

As we passed the location of the restaurant we could see why McDonald's was up in arms, because aside from the different spelling of the name, it had many similarities to the McDonald's one would see elsewhere in the world. The owner didn't seem very concerned about the whole uproar, since the probability of McDonald's representatives traveling all the way to Iraq during a war to push the issue was likely to be slim to none — and so there it sat. The group wondered what they were serving inside, since the security detail didn't really know.

Once again we stopped to walk through the town, visit with the children and take another restroom break. As with the days past the kids were so great to be around, full of smiles and laughter, just as it should be for all children. We then headed by bus to the "Red House."

As we approached the prison it was quickly apparent that the structure had at one time undergone a ferocious firefight.

From the outer walls the site reflected a complex of reddish brown coloring shot full of bullet holes with battle damage everywhere. The old complex was a former torture chamber for Saddam Hussein's regime. In a free Iraq it had been turned into a museum. It was open to the public to share the atrocities that played out in such a facility. We learned our tour guide was well versed on the history of the prison because he had once been a prisoner and torture victim of the Baathist government. He told us he had been imprisoned in the Red House for seven months and tortured for being suspected of knowing information about the Kurdish resistance.

The infamous Red House prison, the site of torture and atrocities handed out by the government of Saddam Hussein.

We were led toward two places of interest. The first was an area where a hole had been blasted through the outer wall into a room. The room was now a nesting area for doves. The guide told us that the doves represented the peace that now prevailed over the facility and the region.

The second place was a room that appeared more modernistic in expression to reflect a dark, almost cave-like environment. The room was dimly lit and the walls and ceilings were covered with broken pieces of mirror. I wasn't sure what the full meaning of the interpretation meant, but I assumed that it represented the dark and evil things that had happened there in the past.

Our guide then led us inside what remained of the prison interior; the place where he and so many other Kurdish nationals had been tortured. As he unlocked the door to the prison one of our group members raised a camera to snap a picture of him. He remarked how ironic it was that the prisoner was now the holder of the keys to the very prison where he had been persecuted. What an interesting observation. As we continued on our tour through the next series of rooms we came face to face with white statue renditions of Soldiers torturing prisoners and of prisoners shackled to the walls.

In another room four statues portrayed two Soldiers holding a pole attached to a prisoner's feet. The prisoner was shown lying on the ground while the Soldiers lifted their feet in the air. Another Soldier held a piece of rubber hose as if he were beating the prisoner's feet.

We were then led into a room where our guide told us how he had been tortured. This room contained only one statue portraying a prisoner with his hands tied together at his wrists. He was hanging from a pole attached to hooks that in turn were attached to the ceiling. As bad as that scene appeared it was actually far worse. The arms of the victim were not raised from the front of his body but from the back — in such a contorted fashion that his arms were dislocated from his shoulder sockets.

Our guide had endured that cruelty for seven months while in captivity. I couldn't fathom having my arms tied behind my back, let alone having them lifted up over my head by my hands. It was an impossible position for anyone to be put in. We had difficulty absorbing what our guide said next. While he was hanging in this agonizing position he was beaten, his genitals were electrocuted and they grabbed him around his body and pulled down further stretching his arms out of their sockets. Behind us he pointed to a generator and a piece of rubber hose that was used to beat the prisoners. After enduring such punishment over several months his shoulders were permanently damaged.

Stunned by what we had learned, we continued down the hall. As we walked our guide noted the wood paneling on the walls that had been installed to help muffle the screams of those being tortured so they couldn't be heard outside on the street. A tactic used to get confessions from the prisoners was to bring a relative in and put them in the room next door. The guards would then torture the relative so that his screams could be heard by the prisoner already suffering from his own excruciating pain — all in an effort to gain a confession. If the prisoner confessed then the Soldiers in the other room would stop torturing their relative.

The entire time our guide was speaking all I could think of was what beasts they were. In the seven months the guide was held prisoner enduring incredible periods of pain, he never once confessed. He was finally let go — but the Baathists continued to closely watch him and his family.

As we wrapped up our tour our guide led us into a prison cell area that was very dark and gray. We noticed drawings and messages left on the walls by former prisoners. The cellblocks were made up of smaller cells with solid steel doors that contained small ports with doors and then a larger cell with bars from floor to ceiling — like an old western jail. The guards would look into the small cells through the ports at night while the prisoners slept — or at least tried to sleep. As the guards made their rounds they would slam the port doors to wake up the prisoners. This went on routinely throughout the night as a method of sleep deprivation — an extension of the torture process.

The large cell with the floor-to-ceiling bars would often hold several prisoners at a time. They were given one small bucket of dirty water to share. To add to the discomfort of their captivity they were only allowed to use the bathroom twice a day. It was difficult not to imagine the smell and the misery of living under such conditions. The rest of the building was a series of empty rooms that we peeked into on our way out.

Outside — fresh air once again! We followed our guide to a courtyard area between the buildings where there were a number of captured Russian military weapons from Saddam's army. There were tanks, armored vehicles, mortar tubes, antiaircraft guns and various kinds of large machine guns all lined up in neat rows. As we passed by I stopped to have my picture taken beside one of the Soviet tanks.

John standing near a Russian tank left over from earlier wars

A short distance away was a concrete observation tower that had been partially destroyed.

The actual hangman's noose used to put prisoners to death at the Red House.

It hung from the main prison wall and touched the ground on the backside. As with much of the outer wall, there were a number of bullet holes and battle damage everywhere. We learned from our guide that in the early 1990s the prison was attacked and recaptured by Kurdish soldiers. During the battle that ensued there was no mercy shown to the Iraqi soldiers who worked at the facility and as a result there were no prisoners taken. They were all killed.

The last building we entered was used for the museum offices and had a few smaller displays. Halls were lined with the pictures of valiant Kurdish fighters who had been executed while housed in the prison. At the end of the hall in a small glass and wood cabinet we saw a hangman's noose that had been used to execute many of them. I was emotionally moved to learn that the brave people reflected in the photos had been killed by hanging to death. Perhaps it was fitting that in the end Saddam Hussein came to know exactly how it felt to have a hangman's noose strung around his own neck.

Our time at the Red House had come to an end, and we exited the building just as the sun was beginning to set in the west. As we walked back to the entrance of the prison I noticed that some of our security detail had tears in their eyes. They told us that they had never toured the prison before, and they were just as touched and moved by the experience as was our group. They were Soldiers too, and as they toured the Red House for the first time we saw the feeling of deep sorrow they had for the suffering endured by their fellow countrymen who had lost their lives in the midst of that torture chamber.

I could empathize with them because I had been on the brink of tears several times that day and completely understood how they felt. One of the last points our guide made as we concluded our visit was how cruel the prison guards were to those who weren't even contained within the prison walls. For example, if a citizen was walking down the outer sidewalk past the prison and they did not look at the ground as they passed, the tower guards would shoot at them, often killing them. In the end, because of the intolerable cruelty of the prison guards when the Kurdish soldiers made their move to recapture the Red House, there were no prisoners taken. All of those Iraqi soldiers met their own demise on that fateful day.

That particular day of all the days on our trip was very emotional and yet at the same time humbling. As we boarded our trusty Mercedes bus to head back to Erbil the mood remained somber. Our route back took a slightly different direction than the way we had arrived. All these years later I assume it was done for security purposes. Regardless, the drive was just as long and it was dark when we finally arrived back within the safety of the hotel grounds.

As everyone else headed into the hotel, I took a few minutes to chat with the head of our security detail. I wanted to thank him for his protection and that of his team. I also asked if he would allow me to take a picture of one of the AK-47s that he had brought along for our safety. After taking my picture I shook his hand and headed into the hotel.

To Iraq and Back

John:

The next morning I spent some quiet time alone in the solace of my room reflecting back on the past eight days of our journey. Along the way I had taken copious notes and plenty of video and pictures. At that moment I couldn't fully understand the impact the trip would have on my life once I returned to the states. I knew my journey to this desolate and forlorn land halfway around the world to find some sense of reason, some sense of peace for Matthew's death was clearly a life-changing event.

In one sense I was completely overwhelmed by the acceptance our group received from a thankful and grateful people. A people who truly could say they understood the burden of pain that my fellow Gold Star parents and I carried with the death of our sons. The next morning would mark the end of our trip. We would return to the comfort and safety of the United States of America — our land of sweet liberty — in some small way healed by the knowledge that our sons did not die in vain. We now had more answers as to why our boys gave their all to save a nation from tyranny.

I packed my notes up and headed downstairs to grab a bite to eat. Our group had been excited the night before to learn we would have the opportunity to play tourists and shop for souvenirs. Before going to an Iraqi bazaar we headed over to the money exchange office in the hotel to become "wealthy" — or at least it felt like that. At the exchange I handed $100 U.S. dollars to the teller and they gave me back the equivalent of about $130,000 Iraqi dollars. It was quite the stack of money. I fanned the bills as if I had won a lottery. After everyone had completed his or her exchange we headed out to the bus for a short drive over to the bazaar.

As with most everything else we had seen over the past eight days it had the air of a place from yesteryear — an ancient version of our own shopping mall. It was totally enclosed but with a tunneling effect and small

125

shops lining both sides. Occasionally we saw exits to the outside, and the tunnels intersected with one another like a crossroads.

Everywhere we looked there were things to buy — rugs, clothes and trinkets of all kinds. I was accompanied and aided by one of the Kurdish officials I had befriended on our trip. I had several purchases in mind, each based on some aspect of our visit. The first purchase consisted of a decorative set of teacups. I wanted to have a reminder of the many cups of tea I was served at each of our meetings with the various officials. Next on my list was a traditional head covering and two different types of Keffiyeh — an Arab head scarf worn by many of the men in the area. The color and design of the Keffiyeh denoted a choice of affiliation with that tribe or family.

My last purchase was for Stacey. Before setting off on our shopping venture I'd decided I wanted to get her a piece of jewelry. I asked my host about the options that were available and he immediately guided me over to an area where one of the vendors sold gold pieces. There was gold everywhere, in fact so much gold that for a moment I thought I'd stepped into Fort Knox. There were solid rings made into bracelets showcased on display racks. I asked my guide why there were so many variations. He explained that when a young man and woman were to be married it was tradition for the groom's family to give a dowry — often in the form of gold jewelry — to the bride on the day of the couple's wedding ceremony. Several bracelets are purchased for each wedding, which is why the gold pieces were so prominently displayed in the windows.

As I gazed at the selections one particular piece caught my eye. I told my friend that I wanted to ask the merchant about a gold link bracelet that I had noticed, and before I knew it negotiations had begun. The merchant shouted out his price, and after counting my money I told my friend that I didn't have enough money. He turned to the merchant and I'm not sure what he said, but the merchant lowered his price. I still didn't have enough Iraqi money to cover the purchase, so I asked the host what the price would be in U.S. dollars. He said $135. I pulled out my wallet to see how much I had in U.S. dollars and asked him how much my remaining Iraqi money was worth in U.S. dollars. By combining the two currencies I had just enough money to buy Stacey the bracelet, with seven dollars left to my name for the rest of the trip.

As I concluded my shopping spree I was pleased because I had really hoped to get Stacey that bracelet. Mission Accomplished. What a day! We wrapped up our shopping and our bus headed back to the memorial park for one last visit.

At the memorial I came across a large granite boulder with the words "Freedom is Not Free" carved into it. Seeing that inscription filled me with emotion because my thoughts immediately turned to Matthew. That particular caption has always touched my heart because of the straightforwardness of a simple but powerful statement. How humbling it was to consider those same words reflected the essence of America's legacy — born in battle and paid for over two centuries by the lives of American service men and women. I had traveled 10,000 miles around the world to this war-ravaged country of Iraq and front and center staring me in the face were the words "Freedom is Not Free!"

Freedom is not Free, a precious message that transcends any language. This monument honors the Iraqis who had lost their lives at the hands of terrorists.

I hope that those who read Matthew's story keep those words etched in their minds, hold them close to their hearts and never forget how precious our freedom truly is. I know I will never forget. And having had the opportunity to gaze into the eyes of so many Iraqi's over the past eight days, I felt assured that they too, will never forget.

After returning to the hotel I went to my room to put away my purchases and freshen up. In a short while our group would be having one of our last meetings with an Iraqi Minister downstairs in the lounge area. As I arrived downstairs, some of them were already listening to the Minister who had come by to talk with us. I sat nearby and listened while the articulate gentleman explained why he believed it was so difficult to gain control of the entirety of Iraq and put an end to the insurgency.

He went on for some time giving one reason after another. I sat quietly along with the others. Not wanting to offend him, I kept hold of my thoughts and feelings. I felt that his words boiled down to a number of menial excuses. After patiently listening I felt compelled to speak my mind. Looking back I recall being rather blunt about why I felt he was wrong. He'd attempted to explain that culturally the government found it very difficult to train and raise an Iraqi Army that was capable of conducting the same level of work effort that the U.S. troops were performing. Hearing that, I jumped into the conversation and told him that in my opinion, "The problem is really quite simple. There are good guys and there are bad guys, and quite frankly the good guys just need to go and get the bad guys." I continued on saying, "You've had two years to get this done, which was more than enough time to train an entire Army."

Prior to traveling to Iraq I'd read that the U.S. Army had trained approximately 300,000 Iraqi troops up to that point. Unfortunately that same article pointed out that once the soldiers completed their training some of them deserted the military. I acknowledged to the Minister that it was understandable there would be problems. Especially given the challenges of preparing a nation to stand up and protect itself after years of widespread oppression. Even so I went on to say, "Why not take the best 50,000 of those trained who truly want to fight for their country and partner them with American Soldiers so they can put their training into action. With those who opt not to fight, take their weapons away and deal with them separately."

He started to reply, but I must admit I cut him off at the pass. Hearing him spew what amounted to plain old excuses made me very upset. I could not believe what I was hearing given that so many young American men and women, as well as Iraqi's and those from the multi-national coalition had already given their lives. I said, "I'm tired of being told what you can't do. I want to hear about what you can do. My son and others like him, me included, went from being a civilian with no experience whatsoever in military protocol to being combat ready, to fight and bear arms in a short eight-week period. Our kids could be deployed into combat after eight weeks of training, and your country has had two years. Take the ones that truly want to fight for their country and send the ones that don't home because they weren't meant for the military anyway."

I also told him that in the United States military if a service member deserted their unit, they were arrested and jailed. Therefore, I would expect no less from the Iraqi military. Our young men and women — our sons and daughters, the best in our nation — had traveled halfway around the world to come to give the Iraqi's a hand up, and for that, many had lost their lives. In the end I said, "The American public will not tolerate this forever and God help you if we leave and you are not willing to stand on your own."

As I recall, I left the Minister momentarily speechless. The others who were listening were equally as silent. But I had said my piece. Reflecting back on my notes, perhaps, what I'd said expressed my anger in the circumstances as I saw it. Nonetheless I'd needed to share my feelings.

That evening we had our final dinner at the hotel. About fifteen other Kurdish officials joined us as well. There was plenty of food to go around, and everyone joined in a local tradition of smoking a hookah pipe which was quite interesting. A hookah tender offered us a water pipe or "hookah", and then a flavor of tobacco was selected. The tender packed the bowl of the water pipe with the tobacco and then put a screen on top of it. Once the screen was in place, hot coals were placed on top to heat the tobacco. Each person was given his or her own colored mouthpiece and took turns puffing on the pipe. It was quite hilarious to watch, and not at all like cigarette smoking. While it appeared as if the smoker made tons of smoke, he really didn't feel the effects of it, like one would the drag on a cigarette. Unfortunately I knew from experience because after learning of Matthew's death I'd returned to smoking cigarettes, a habit I had kicked years before. Quite frankly I didn't see the purpose of the hookah, but that evening after some pretty tense pre-dinner conversation it was good for some badly needed laughs.

As we prepared to order our meal, some of us headed outside to the back of the restaurant where the live fish were kept to make our dinner selection and to watch them cook the traditional flat bread in a primitive stone oven. It was oriented with the opening at the top, sort of like a chimney. The bread maker cooked the flatbread by reaching in through the top to stick the dough to the side of the oven.

As I watched the process I thought how hot it must have been to stick ones hand in that oven, because once the bread was inside it cooked fairly quickly. When it was done the cook stuck his hand back in the oven and peeled the bread off the side, threw it onto the pile with the rest of the flatbread and started the process all over again, moving very quickly in an effort not to burn their hands. After watching the cook go through his steps several times, I decided it wasn't something I was willing to try.

While we were gathered behind the restaurant, four professional looking Kurdish soldiers came walking up. When I say professional I don't mean nicely dressed. They looked like combat hardened U.S. troops, guys that looked as if they could handle themselves very comfortably. Each one carried an AK-47. They were amicable and openly conversing amongst the guests. Those of us from our group who had congregated in the back thanked them for their service. Given the exchange earlier in the evening with the Minister, that would become another remembrance for me — one I hold to this day.

The rest of our evening went by quickly, ending as so many over the past eight days, gathered in the hotel lounge talking. That evening the conversation centered on what each of us had experienced and would take away from this trip. The next day we would be homeward bound after spending the past ten days on a journey to Iraq and back home.

Homeward Bound

John:

Today marks the tenth day of our journey. As normal, I was awake pretty early. I spent some quiet time reflecting back on the past nine days as I packed my bags and showered. After getting dressed I headed downstairs to meet up with the rest of our group and check out of the hotel.

While we waited for the signal to board the bus for Erbil airport, we reminisced about the things we had seen and the opportunities we were given while in Iraq. We were saddened by the fact that it was all over much too soon, but excited about getting back home to our loved ones. We looked forward to having the honor of sharing with others in the United States the great things that our children, our heroes, had been able to accomplish in aiding the Iraqi people in rebuilding their country and standing up a democracy.

During our visit I had commented a number of times to our Iraqi hosts that our nation did not come to do all of the work for them. Rather we were, as they said, liberators. People willing to help others do the things they weren't able to do until they could help themselves. The United States could arrest or kill all the terrorists in Iraq, but if the Iraqis weren't willing to stand up and fight for their own people, there wasn't anything else we could do to help them.

Once on the bus we went at the usual high rate of speed to avoid trouble, making our way back to the airport where our adventure had begun just seven days before. As before, we had to surrender our passports and wait in the secured area. We sat quietly, exhausted, drinking the traditional tea while we waited for our flight to Amman, Jordan.

After our bags were taken care of we waited to board the plane. My thoughts drifted to the long trip ahead of me. I would be flying back to San Diego via Dallas, Texas where I would meet up with Stacey.

Prior to my travel plans to Iraq we had been contacted by the American Legion post in The Colony, Texas. Our family had spent seven years living in The Colony from 1992 to 1999, and the American Legion wanted to honor us by renaming Post 21 after Matthew and Jimmy Riddle, another veteran and American Hero who had given his life while conducting security training as a contractor in Iraq. The dedication ceremony and unveiling was scheduled in conjunction with Veterans Day and hosted by the newly name Holley-Riddle American Legion Post 21. I had been asked to be a guest speaker at the event, and it was important for me to be there. Both Stacey and I were truly honored that the town thought enough of Matthew to consider him in the naming of the Post.

Finally, the time arrived for us to board "Jessica" the aircraft that had brought us to Iraq. As we slowly headed out to the runway I was both glad to be heading home and sad to be leaving the land where Matthew had spent his last hours of life on earth. During the time I'd spent in Iraq I made some close friendships with some of the security personnel, and I wondered how they would fair through the rest of the war.

Reflecting back, I knew I had been given the opportunity of a lifetime to see and do some amazing things. In some strange way I found solace in knowing I'd accomplished what I had traveled over 10,000 miles from home to do. I felt satisfied that I had honored Stacey, our family and especially our son Matthew. The plane took off without delay, and before I knew it we were once again landing in Amman, Jordan.

There would be a couple of tense moments after entering the terminal and proceeding through security to board the next flight to London. I walked across the tarmac with the rest of the passengers, entered the terminal to wait in the security line, and the first one unfolded before me. Ahead of me in line were what appeared to be two private U.S. Military contracted security personnel. They sported short-cropped haircuts and wore desert combat boots and fatigue pants with desert-like tan t-shirts.

One of the gentlemen was told by the security personnel that they wanted to search his backpack. What appeared to be a routine request given the region of the world we were in, seemed to make him very agitated, to the point that he began arguing with the Jordanian military official.

As I listened to the exchange I thought, *Do you know where you are?* After all, we weren't in America yet, we were still in the Middle East!

Several minutes passed before the backpack was returned to the security contractor and he continued on his way in a huff. How lucky for him. I wasn't sure what the inside of a Jordanian prison was like, but it's probably fair to say he wouldn't have liked it.

I was next to step up to the security desk, and after what I had just witnessed I decided it was probably best to be as polite as possible. As the Jordanian official began to inspect my carryon bag he pulled out my cell phone. In his best English he asked, "What is this?" to which I replied, "My cell phone." I was puzzled by his question and equally so as he began to carefully inspect the phone. After a moment passed, he stepped away to summon another of his colleagues.

In short order a very official looking gentleman appeared wearing an equally impressive uniform and an even more impressive hat. I assumed he was a superior officer, or perhaps the officer in charge of the security personnel. The soldier, who was inspecting my phone, handed it over to his superior who studied it as well. He stopped for a moment to look at me, and then asked me what I did with the phone.

The question puzzled me — it just seemed like a strange query — but I responded with the only answer I knew, "I make personal phone calls with it."

As he continued to inspect the phone, I became concerned, wondering if I was about to lose possession of my phone. The phone contained all of my contact files.

Another minute passed as he continued looking the phone over. Then he asked me if making calls was all I did with it, to which I replied "Yes, I just make calls on it." He continued looking at it for a few more minutes and then handed it back to me commenting, "We don't like these phones." The other soldier handed me my bag, and I placed my phone back in it and proceeded through the checkpoint.

Afterwards as I thought about the encounter I was puzzled. But after giving it some thought I realized the reason for their concern. The particular phone I owned had a push-to-talk capability, which I suspected might have been connected with the type of cell phones used to detonate IEDs. After arriving back in the U.S., my suspicions would be confirmed. I learned that phones similar to the one I owned could be placed on an IED and then signaled by another push-to-talk device causing the explosive to detonate.

It sure was a relief that I had been allowed to clear the security checkpoint with my phone in hand. I headed upstairs to meet up with the remainder of the Gold Star parents. A few of the others in our group had left the day before, and so I shook hands and gave hugs to the remaining team and we parted ways.

In just one short week we would be reunited in Washington D.C. for a scheduled press conference. The conference had been planned prior to our leaving the states so that we could share the "good news" about the accomplishments that our sons and their fellow service members had made.

After our goodbyes I headed over to the gate for my flight to London. After boarding the flight and settling into my seat I noticed that I was seated next to an Egyptian gentleman. He was friendly, and we talked for a few minutes. Shortly after takeoff I promptly fell asleep. I really don't remember much about the flight or even how long I slept. I was exhausted.

The flight was uneventful other than the fact that our plane was delayed arriving into London, which didn't help matters. I was stressed because I was a on a tight timeline to arrive in Dallas for the Veterans Day ceremony.

I exited the plane and rushed to pick up my bag in customs. From there I literally ran for the ticket counter to recheck my bag and see if I could make the next leg of my flight. Unfortunately, luck wasn't on my side and I wasn't able to clear security in time to catch the originally scheduled flight. I returned to the ticket counter distressed, completely exhausted and pretty emotional. All that was on my mind was getting to Dallas.

The ticket agent recognizing my frustration worked diligently to book me on the next available flight, which was due to leave two hours later. However, that connection would get me into New York that evening, with the final leg scheduled to leave New York for Dallas the following morning. I would have an eight-hour layover in New York. I told myself to relax because my new arrangements would still have me arriving in Dallas with just enough time to get to the ceremonies and share our story.

Finally, I heard the announcement for me to board the plane from London to New York. Once airborne the flight was fairly smooth and uneventful. Roughly eight hours later I landed back on U.S. soil. We landed at New York's JFK airport around midnight.

After clearing customs I headed off to find a bus or cab as my flight the next morning would be leaving from LaGuardia, which was about thirty minutes from JFK. By that point exhaustion was starting to take hold. I had now been traveling for nearly thirty hours, and I was absolutely worn out.

Much of what I encountered on that trip home was relatively new for me. I was somewhat familiar with traveling internationally, but not as accustomed to taking cabs or scheduling and rescheduling flights. I rarely traveled without Stacey, and she was far more comfortable maneuvering the morass of travel venues then I. Coupled with the exhaustion and the overall strangeness of my surroundings, I was somewhat uneasy.

I finally made it to LaGuardia and dragged myself into the terminal, feeling literally half dead and realizing after nearly thirty hours without bathing that I probably didn't smell too good either. I longed for a shower, a change of clothes, some food and especially a very large cup of real American coffee.

By now my clothes were plastered to me, and to top it off the airport was essentially closed except for the outer part of the terminal. From what I could tell there wasn't even a single place to get food, "Ugh!" With bag in tow I found the nearest men's room and attempted to clean myself up as best as possible, which included changing my clothes. While that helped me feel a tad better, my fatigue was extreme and unfortunately it wasn't going to get any easier. I faced a dilemma. While I desperately needed sleep, I was fearful of missing my flight to Dallas that was scheduled to leave first thing in the morning. Additionally, I was jumpy about my belongings being taken if I dozed off. So over the next several hours I did just about everything I could creatively think of to stay awake and alert. I wandered the airport hallways, sat occasionally for short periods of time, stopped by the men's room at other times to splash my face with cold water — anything to make sure I didn't miss that flight. Along the way I observed several other people like myself wandering around to stay awake, except for one gentleman that couldn't hang with rest of us zombies. He was probably the smartest of all of us, because he chose instead to sleep.

And then just like in "The Star-Spangled Banner" I was able to behold the dawn's early light. As the sun began to rise outside, the airport slowly came to life inside. Around 7 a.m. I was able to get some breakfast and that much needed cup of coffee. Still in that ever-present zombie state I made my way through security and headed down to my gate for Texas. A feeling of absolute relief came upon me as I proceeded to take the last leg of my journey home to my beautiful wife.

By the time we landed I had thirty minutes to spare before I would stand up to speak at the pending Veteran's Day ceremonies. After clearing security I headed for the airport exit in search of my brother-in-law, Kreig. Stacey had arranged for him to meet me. We quickly shook hands and he welcomed me back to the states as we hurried to his truck for the short drive to The Colony. We made it to the ceremony with literally minutes to spare, and before anything else I sought out Stacey and gave her the biggest hug I could.

I had just completed a nearly forty-hour journey that took me from the city center of Erbil, Iraq to Dallas, Texas on very little sleep. I was exhausted, but there was nothing I was more prepared to do then share my heart and our son with several hundred residents and dignitaries. I was quickly introduced to those coordinating the speakers, and shown to my seat on the stage where I awaited my turn to address the audience.

When it came my time to speak I rose and through bloodshot eyes I delivered a message that was both emotionally charged and tear filled. Many in the audience cried with me as I spoke of Matthew and his sacrifice for his country and what a tribute it was for the American Legion Post 21 of The Colony to honor Matthew's sacrifice - to honor an American Hero.

I was the last speaker, and following the conclusion of my speech the ceremony continued as the Post 21 members presented the American flag to both Stacey and Mrs. Riddle, along with a replica granite plaque with an etched picture of both Matthew and Jimmy. The original plaques would reside at the Post location.

Once the ceremonies concluded Stacey and I spoke with many of those in attendance including several old friends from our years spent in Texas and with other family members. After most had left we joined some very close friends that lived in Dallas for a cup of coffee. Within the hour Stacey noticed I was fading quickly and we said our goodbyes, none too soon.

Recalling the trip I took I'm blessed in knowing I had an opportunity to do what so many other Gold Star parents have wanted to do as well. That was to go to the land where their sons or daughters had given their lives to offer freedom to an oppressed nation. Strangely, I had no qualms or fear of going into a war torn country in the throes of combat — after all, my son had done the same. It was clearly the adventure of a lifetime, and not a responsibility I took lightly. In so many ways it was exactly what I needed to help me begin to heal my heart, my mind and my soul.

I will forever miss the hero that Stacey and I raised to be a man of principle, a man who understood the meaning of serving a cause much greater than self. I had an opportunity to stare into the faces of a people who were grateful for the sacrifices of the best our nation had to give, forever grateful that because their fellow man stood for them in their hour of need, they could one day learn to stand for themselves. Right or wrong, in my mind it had been something I needed to do despite the risk involved.

Our New Walk — Finding Strength

John:

As Stacey and I have alluded to several times, this walk — this journey — has been trying for the both of us, emotionally, physically, and mentally. We've all heard people say that they wouldn't wish their worst nightmare on anyone. I can honestly say that neither of us would ever wish the pain of losing a child on another parent.

The hurt we've endured has been unbearable at times, even years after the fact. And yet we've come to accept that it's a burden we will carry the rest of our lives. As I reflect on this, I realize that for those who suffer such pain, there are really only two options...

Imagine for a moment that you were walking down the path of your life and suddenly without any warning you stumbled into a deep pit. At that point you would have a few choices, a few options to turn your circumstances around. You could continue sitting at the bottom of that pit, nursing your anger, feeling sorry for yourself, and moaning about your misfortune. You could refuse the help of anyone who tried to lift you out of the pit or — worse yet — you could simply decide to stay there, and see how many people you could drag down with you. In the end you'd be doing no one any good, least of all yourself.

The second option is a bit more obvious... You could choose to crawl out of the pit. Perhaps you'd be able to make it out under your own power, or perhaps you would require the help of others. Either way, doesn't really matter. The important thing would be to do whatever you needed to do to get out of the pit; to fight with all your might to get back to level ground — a place where you could learn to stand on your own once again.

I said that the second option would be the obvious choice. You'll notice that I didn't say it would be the easiest. Crawling out of that pit may turn out to be the hardest thing you ever do, but it may also be the most important.

Once you're back on the path again, look carefully around yourself. You may find that other people have fallen into the pit. And you may

discover that your struggle back to level ground has made you stronger —
it's given you a strength and grace to carry a burden you never imagined
you could carry. You may even find the strength to reach down into the
pit, and help others climb back into the light.

As we've shared our hearts through the words in this book, I hope
you'll see that Stacey and I have dedicated ourselves to lifting others out
of the pit. We've been down there in that dark abyss. We know how
frightening and hopeless that pit can seem, and how far away the light can
be. But — above all else — we learned the way out, and we're determined
to help others find their way out as well.

We've chosen to live by a simple lesson, one of those lessons in life
that we learned many years ago — one that Stacey has already spoken
about in the earlier pages of this book. Be willing to take your eyes off of
yourself, and put them onto others. It's the same lesson that Matthew
applied in his chosen profession.

As we taught our son, we too needed to learn that — through our pain
— we can reach out to help others. We can touch the lives of other people,
even while we're experiencing our own traumas. It's truly humbling to
realize how many other people are in pain. By offering to help them,
we've come to learn that we can diminish our own pain, our own
suffering.

In the years that have passed I find myself thinking about a car accident
that occurred near Spokane, Washington just about two weeks before
Matthew was killed. A father driving his family home at the end of a long
day was involved in a head-on collision. The father survived the crash, but
all five of his children were killed.

As Stacey and I have shared our story over the past several years,
people have often commented that they can't imagine what it's like to
experience the pain of losing a child. We don't have to imagine it. Stacey
and I know exactly how it feels. But even we cannot imagine what it must
feel like to lose five children in a single night.

In 2008, the driver who caused that dreadful crash went on trial, and the
accident found its way back onto the front page of the Spokane
newspapers. I'm not sure I ever learned what caused his vehicle to veer
into oncoming traffic. I can't remember the mechanics of the accident, and
I've long since forgotten most of the details. Even so, there's one part of
the story that will stay with me forever. I will never forget the healing and
forgiveness that came out of that tragedy.

The father of the five children spoke publicly about the ordeal that he
and his wife had undergone. Even so, in the depths of their grief, they
reached out to the family of the other driver extending their forgiveness

and their prayer. Shattered and stunned by the intensity of their loss, they did not know what to ask of God, so they kept their prayer simple. "Thy will be done, Lord."

They didn't know what the future held in store for them. They couldn't make any sense of their loss. They had no answers — only questions. So they turned to their creator. "Thy will be done, Lord." In their deepest moments of pain they had taken their eyes off of themselves, and put them onto others.

The accident was horrific, and the loss and suffering that it caused was incomprehensible. But each family in this tragedy had a choice — the pit, or level ground. As difficult as it must have been, the two families chose wisely. By the grace of God, they are on level ground.

Once, another mother said to us, "At least your son died honorably. He died for something. My child died from a drug overdose." It was comforting that this grieving parent chose to honor Matthew's memory. Yet, at the same time it was heartbreaking to imagine the pain of losing a child to something as senseless as drug abuse. There are so many senseless tragedies in this world — murders, kidnappings, rapes — and many more crimes too vile to imagine.

As human beings, we want the world to make sense. We try to understand crimes and accidents, and catastrophes, even when there's no conceivable reason for them. We want to know why such misfortunes are inflicted upon us. We want to point our finger at someone, to lay the blame at someone's feet.

For Stacey and me it would have been very easy to point our accusing finger at God. After all, He made the world. He created the human race. He could end all suffering with a wave of His hand. It's His entire fault. It *must* be His fault.

But is it? I thought about it for a moment. Is any of this really God's fault? He gave us free will. If he hadn't given us *choice*, we'd all be like little puppets, dancing on the end of his strings. So he gave us the power to *choose*. We can help each other, or hurt each other. We can do good, or we can do evil. The choice is really *ours*, and what we do with that choice is our own responsibility.

I don't blame God for what happened to Matthew. It's not God's fault. God does not go around 'zapping' people out of their boots. If he did, I'd feel certain that there would never have been a Hitler, a Stalin, Pol Pot, a Mussolini or any of the thousands of vicious criminals who have walked this earth since time began.

I do believe that it is the responsibility of each of us to relieve as much suffering as we can. If every person did just a little to help out another human being, we could relieve so much suffering in the world.

It's easy to get so wrapped up in our own lives that we can't see beyond our personal problems, but that shouldn't be an excuse. Whether it's monetary help or physical assistance, or just a listening ear and a supportive shoulder we all have something to offer.

"Do unto others as you would have them do unto you." They used to teach this in our public schools. It was known as the Golden Rule and — if we applied it on a regular basis — I honestly believe that the world would be a more pleasant place to live.

Stacey and I have made it our new mission in life to reach out and help as many people as we can. Do we think we can help everyone? Of course not! God has graced us with the strength to make a difference in the lives of other people.

We began even before Matthew's funeral. At the suggestion of a close friend, we invited people to send donations instead of flowers as a remembrance to Matthew. Our hope was to use the monies collected for charitable purposes. From that initial outpouring, coupled with contributions of our own, Stacey and I started The Matthew Holley Foundation (www.matthewholleyfoundation.com), dedicated to helping high school aged children with scholarship monies to inspire their pursuit in the arts and academics. Since 2006 The Matthew Holley Foundation, a California nonprofit foundation has awarded a number of scholarship awards to high school seniors intending to further their education at the collegiate level.

The foundation's Warrior Spirit award has gone to the top male and female competitors at the AAU Pacific Southwest Regional Karate tournament, a qualifier for the national competition. This award honors Matthew's love of the martial arts and his achievements as a three-time U.S. National AAU Karate Champion.

The Excellence Award has gone to the top JROTC cadet in The Colony, Texas near Dallas - where we lived for seven years. In 2006 the American Legion Post 21 in The Colony, Texas renamed their Post 21 the Holley/Riddle Post 21 in honor of Matthew Holley and Jimmy Riddle, two local heroes who died for their country.

The third award is the Patriot Spirit Award that has gone to a top student leader attending Ocean View Christian Academy in San Diego, where Matthew attended in his early years. The areas considered for the Excellence and Patriot Spirit awards are based on academic achievement, leadership and community service.

Matthew dearly loved both the martial and graphic arts, and he had an especially big heart to serve the youth. Stacey and I believe that Matthew would be pleased to be remembered in this way.

The act of helping others has helped us, too. It has given us encouragement and a motivation to carry on — to put one step in front of another — to press forward. We get out of bed every morning knowing that there is always more to do. We move forward through life extending our hands whenever possible, always looking for the chance to lift someone up and out of their pit. As painful as this journey has been, we keep moving forward, sharing our hearts with the strength of God behind us, and with Jesus as our example — showing us the way.

Over the past several years we've been blessed with opportunities to speak to audiences across the country. We realize that every such opportunity is a gift, and we've done our best to help our listeners benefit from our walk in life.

I've been to Walter Reed Hospital, to visit and talk with our wounded warriors. I had one conversation with a young man who endured nine IED attacks before the tenth attack knocked him out of action with a head injury. He had served in the 101st Airborne Division, and had deployed with Matthew, back in October 2005. That connection made his story very personal to me. He and Matthew weren't assigned to the same brigade, but they were brothers nonetheless.

Stacey and I have spoken to many parents who have walked in our shoes. We've shared our experiences with them, and we've shared some of the hard-won lessons that have helped us through our pain. We've received numerous letters, cards, and emails in return, thanking us for the encouragement we've provided. And every time we lend someone a shoulder or a hand, we find that we're helping ourselves all over again.

We will speak to anyone who needs us. If our words or our hearts can help someone, we will do it. That was the impetus behind writing this book. A lesson is only useful if you remember it and share it. A story is only helpful if you share it. That's our hope, and our dream. If we share our hearts openly, it may inspire others to climb out of their pit of despair, and back on to level ground.

On this journey, we feel the greatest impact we've had on the lives of others was the work we did to pursue the passage of The Holley Provision. So many people have told us that the provision has gone a long way toward easing their pain, by giving them an appropriate final memory of their fallen hero or heroine. It's important for parents, spouses and other loved ones to begin the grieving process properly by knowing that their warriors have been properly recognized.

Jesus said, "Greater love has no one than this that he lay down his life for his friends." Our fallen warriors have done this. They have laid down their lives for their friends, for their nation, and for their fellow men. Their sacrifices deserve to be honored. In short, that is what The Holley Provision is all about.

If we had not done these things; if we hadn't taken our eyes off of ourselves and put them onto others, we could not have begun to heal our broken hearts. Yet even though time has softened our pain, we carry a deep scar that will never go away. We are stronger now, and we are getting better at bearing our grief, but it never completely stops taking its toll. It has affected our daily lives, our marriage and our relationships with other people.

My hope in sharing these final thoughts is to fill in some of the gaps with additional insight and deeper reflection of our walk these past several years. It's difficult not to reflect back on 2005, as it was clearly a life-changing year in so many ways. On one front Stacey and I had relocated to the Pacific Northwest to pursue our personal interests and to enjoy the fruits of our labor.

Success had come to us in so many ways, and we felt truly blessed. Because of our efforts we were in a position to move north to be closer to family and spend time with Stacey's ailing father and to help her mother. Then in the quietness of a cool fall day the ring of the doorbell at our North Idaho home on November 16 brought our world crashing down around us. One of my closest friends in life, the young man I had been given the honor of raising, was gone in an instant and from that point on life as we knew it would forever change. Never in a million years would I have dreamed that Stacey and I could have done so many things without something far greater than us guiding our steps. Our faith by far is what has sustained us through a very tumultuous time of our married life.

After the initial visits to Washington D.C. for the press conferences following my trip to Iraq, I was given a couple of more opportunities to make additional trips to the bastion of freedom for our country. The goal during those visits was to lend support to the mission our nation had undertaken. The mission to defeat those who wished our country harm in the War on Terror and to show support for those who continued to serve in our Armed Forces.

During one of those early trips I was honored to give a speech at the Vietnam Veterans Memorial at an event called The Gathering of Eagles in conjunction with Rolling Thunder, an annual gathering of Vietnam Veterans in Washington, D.C. In 2007 this event was put together as a counter protest to the demonstrations of anti-war organizations. That first trip will always be in my memory because of the bitter cold, windy, icy day that we awoke to. Regardless of the weather conditions when I arrived to speak at the event it was clear that our veterans were there in full force to the tune of tens of thousands. I, along with the other speakers scheduled that day, hunkered down and endured to speak from our hearts.

I couldn't help to be inspired, seeing the faces of so many American heroes who were there to support one another, to honor our fallen heroes and to support those who were still serving. As was often the case in those early days, when it came my turn to speak, I choked up, and yet through those tears I delivered my message. I looked at a few faces in the crowd, and they had tears as well. That day will always stand out as one of the most memorable days of my life.

The evening prior to the event I sat down to pen the words I wanted to say; words of honor and thanks. But most of all I wanted to share my son, my hero, a Screaming Eagle! The following is a copy of the speech I gave that day:

Gathering of Eagles, March 17, 2007

Speech by John M. Holley

"I'm honored to be here today at this Gathering of Eagles because what I see before me is a small but mighty sample of United Americans. Since the outset of this war I have been troubled by the division in this country. I can't understand why, when our loved ones are in harm's way we as Americans find it hard to come together in a common cause — the cause to liberate an oppressed people that were subjected to murder, torture and genocide.

Back in November 2006 a small group of Gold Star parents myself included embarked on a trip to Iraq to see for ourselves the land that our loved ones had fought and died for to liberate. We went there to smell the air, to meet the people, and to walk a mile in our sons' shoes! And, what I found when I went there was a good story, a story of hope, the hope of what could be for the whole of Iraq.

The Iraqis we met thank America for their freedom — they call us liberators. They grieve for our loss as they grieve for the ones that they've lost. I saw the tears of a mother as she held up the photos of the sons she had lost. And, I saw the smiles of the children as they crowded around to meet the Americans who had come to visit. These are the Iraqi children that my son had wanted to teach to draw with crayons that I was going to send but never got the chance too.

Specialist Matthew John Holley, Combat Medic, 101st Airborne Division told his mother before joining the military that he was joining "To serve a cause greater than himself." That's the character of these men and woman that serve in our armed forces today. They volunteered to do their chosen profession, and to do it proudly. They were not forced to join, they did it willingly.

My son and all the men and women who have served this nation did so to protect and defend us from enemies foreign or domestic, and we are here today to stand against a domestic enemy bent on a cut and run strategy that will end up causing the deaths of more people than they can imagine and desecrate the memory of those that laid down their lives for their fellow man in this war.

I believe that the soil our loved ones bled upon is hallowed ground and to leave would be an abomination. I would say to these voices that want to cut and run, "You — You go to Iraq like I and my fellow Gold Star Parents did and look into the eyes of the children and tell them, "You're not worth saving." These children are the future of Iraq and when they grow up what will they think of an American who cut and ran when they needed us most.

Lastly, I would like to close with a quote from Horace Mann. He said, "Be ashamed to die if you do nothing to help your fellow man." And I stand here before you as one American who is unashamed to die, and by your presence here you shouldn't be either.

Thank You and God Bless you all."

Another trip to Washington D.C. in the middle of 2007 was once again focused on showing support for our troops and to lobby Congress as a contingent of Gold Star parents to not cut and run on the war in Iraq. It is my belief that most people don't understand that as terrible as war is, we really had only two choices. Either we choose to fight the terrorists on our soil or we can fight them on theirs. Regardless, people would be killed or injured and there would be emotional upheaval as the people wondered why someone didn't do something to stop those who wished to destroy our country. Either way, American lives would be lost, but potentially far fewer would die if we took the fight to their soil. Keep in mind World War II has been over sixty years and we still have troops in both Germany and Japan. Sometimes it could literally be as simple as applying the golden rule, *Love thy Neighbor as Thyself*, and by doing so perhaps we wouldn't have to experience the pain of war.

These days it's not unusual to spend hours in deep thought about how things could have been; Matthew would be twenty-six years old at the completion of this writing. Perhaps he would have been married — perhaps with a child of his own — our grandchild. I envision myself bouncing grandchildren on my knees singing my little song that I made up for Matthew when he was a baby. "Ride the little horsy round and round, oops little horsy don't fall down." Even as I write this it brings a smile to my heart, remembering Matthew's laughter, and yes I feel that pressure in my throat. On the oops little horsy part I would always let him drop a couple of inches off my knees and then lift him back up and do it all over again. He would laugh every time.

There is no doubt that as his parents Stacey and I are very proud of his many accomplishments, especially his talent as a gifted artist and his athletic discipline shown as a three-time U.S. AAU National Karate Champion. We treasure the memories of watching him train the younger kids at the dojo; he was always so good with children. Perhaps it was for that reason that I tried to steer him to become an art teacher. He was so much more patient then I ever was, and I felt he would have been very good at teaching kids. But in the end he chose one of the oldest professions known to man — *Soldier*! To add to it, he chose to be a Combat Medic because he wanted to help others. Then add to that his desire to choose to serve with the storied 101st Airborne Division and earn his Air Assault wings just like his father had done all those years ago in 1978.

On this journey I've come to understand the emotions of a combat veteran because I was a Soldier once too. The experience of losing one of my best friends in my son, and then stepping foot in the war zone of Iraq, right down to the Post Traumatic Stress Disorder (PTSD). In the early days of our grief I would say that on November 16, 2005 I died and woke up to a much different version of John Holley. Oh sure, I looked the same, but my mind did not function the same. I've read that severe trauma or PTSD can change one's brain chemically, and I can honestly say I believe that, because I've lived with it. I have come to accept that grief is like a virus running in the background of our mind, ever present, resistant, crashing our system at random times.

The one constant for Stacey and me through all of this has been the need to reach out and help others — to touch their lives in some small way — to take our eyes off of our own pain and focus on others. This is what we feel we've been called to dedicate the rest of our lives too. Stacey and I are purpose driven people and for the greater part of his twenty-one years on earth Matthew was our greatest purpose.

Now that he isn't here with us, we feel it's our responsibility to be the best husband and wife we can be and to help parents walk this path as best they can. The start of that process for us was the passage of The Holley Provision, which was done out of respect for our fallen heroes and to ensure a proper and lasting memory for their family members. This journey has its fair share of sad memories, and that was one that they didn't need to live with. As sad and painful as this walk has been for Stacey and me, I know there are others who have journeyed through life with far worse burdens to carry.

Reflecting back on my journey to Iraq brought that front and center. Thinking about all the children and adults that have been murdered or died senselessly, and for what? For anyone experiencing similar pain, I'm sorry for your loss. I understand what you are going through.

I recently coined a phrase that brings me some perspective. *No one gets through this life without a scar.* Another saying that expresses the same sentiment of how much worse life could be is, *I used to complain that I had no shoes until I met a man who had no feet.* It could always be much worse and it's not so much what happens to us, it's what we do about it to continue positively touching other people along the way, and perhaps most importantly to know that ultimately God is in complete control. I heard Stacey share a beautiful thought that I tend to agree with it. A thought based on a passage of scripture from John 15:13, Jesus said, *Greater love has no one than this, that he lay down his life for his friends.* From this, Stacey derived that there is a special place in heaven for Soldiers, for those who are willing to lay down their lives for their friends, and for their fellow man. My hope is that our story will bring comfort to those who grieve.

From a Mother's Heart

<u>Stacey</u>:

John came up with a saying that hits the nail on the head. *No one gets through life without a scar*, and to that I add *some scars are just deeper than others*. We have both shared the same journey, yet — in many ways — we've walked very different paths, both physically and emotionally. Sometimes, when John is up, I will be down and sometimes, it's the other way around. Regardless of those ups and downs, this passage has been trying, draining, and stressful.

I've heard it said that there is no greater strain on a marriage then enduring the death of a child. It wasn't just a child for John and me. Matthew was our only child. He was our beautiful son, at the prime of his life and just setting out to make his mark on the world. He was our best friend.

What is our identity without our mutual best friend? What can you do when you've built your life around another person, and that person is suddenly taken away? We're discovering the answers to those questions a little bit at a time.

Along the way, a few of our closest friends have reached out to us, and provided us with insight and advice. One incredibly useful bit came very early on, from a very dear friend who told us — quite correctly — that our grieving processes might not look the same. John's grief might be quite different from mine, and that it was important for both of us to understand that neither his way nor my way would be right, or wrong. We needed to respect and support one another, regardless of our personal opinions about how to show grief, or cope with it.

Being together twenty-six years at the time of Matthew's death had given us a strong foundation to stand on. That, along with our faith in God, allowed us to rise out of that pit John referred to and walk on level ground.

I can't claim that our struggles have become effortless, and it's still not easy to talk about or even to put these words on paper. But I can say that this walk we're on has given us new strength. We've also taken strength from those who have walked beside us along the way. Some have walked with us for a moment, and some for a season. There are others who have promised to stand beside us for as long as we need them, even if it takes a lifetime. We've been encouraged by these friendships, and by the way they have strengthened both our family, and our faith.

In death, our son taught us what many search a lifetime for, that each of us possesses an incredible strength and grace that only God has given us.

Ecclesiastes tells us there is a purpose and reason for everything that happens on this journey we call life. I tend to believe that nothing happens by chance, or by luck, whether good or bad. In life everyone endures some kind of suffering whether by illness or injury, hurts or love, or even lost moments of greatness. Whatever the circumstances, each of us will be tested to the depths and limits of our soul.

If we could see these trials approaching, we would probably run to avoid them. It's natural to bypass difficulty and suffering when we can. But I have come to believe that such tests give our lives shape and purpose. Without them our lives might become straight, flat roads to nowhere. Our existence might be safe and comfortable, but it would also be dull and utterly pointless.

Personally, I happen to believe in purpose as does John. At times we've crossed paths with others who were meant to be a part of our lives. Some of these people have come to teach us lessons, offer a shoulder to lean on, or help us understand who we are and what we might become. Our lives have been touched by neighbors, teachers, relatives, business associates, long lost friends, and even complete strangers. Upon meeting each of these people, we somehow knew that they would affect our lives in some profound way.

I think it's a mistake to discount the unpleasant parts of our lives. It's tempting to want to forget or deny the difficult and painful things that have happened to us. Yet only in hindsight can we see how important those trials are. It's by overcoming those obstacles placed in our path that we come to realize our full potential. To conquer adversity we must gather our willpower, and our inner strength. To move forward we must become better, stronger, wiser and more confident.

We learn from our successes, but we also learn from our downfalls. When we are in the midst of a personal tragedy, it can be hard to recognize the value of what we are gaining, but the value is there nonetheless. As heartbreaking as they may be, our challenges help us to become the people we were meant to be.

*   *   *

As John mentioned earlier, we have learned to measure ourselves against a new and higher standard. It reminds us that as long as we are blessed to live on this earth, we must make every day count.

We have discovered within ourselves the power to touch the lives of other people. We must try to appreciate every moment and take from it everything that we possibly can.

We must be willing to talk to people we have never talked to before, and to lend them a listening ear. We must learn to see past our fears. We must trust ourselves to fly knowing that sometimes we will fall.

God has told us that we can be more than we are. Jesus came to this world to prove to us that it's possible. And our son Matthew has shown us that we can live up to the higher self within each of us.

That's the standard we must measure ourselves against, to find our inner angels. We can do it, and we will. We are determined to become what we are meant to be.

Seven thousand, seven hundred and twenty two — that's the number of days John and I were blessed to have Matthew in our lives on this earth. There aren't many days that go by that this thought doesn't cross my mind, and as it does I'm reminded of the movie *Gladiator* that brings to the forefront the thoughts I have as I close — *Strength and Honor*.

Those who choose to serve our nation carry a burden to do so, to make a difference in the lives of others. War is not glorious in any way shape or form. It is perhaps the ugliest side of humanity, and at the same time it can be one of the most honoring. It is man who starts it and man who can end it. It brings tears to the hearts of many and scars that carry with them painful reminders; scars to the heart, mind and soul. It tests the very fiber of our emotional fabric.

As a mother it was extremely difficult to understand why my precious Matthew chose this path in life. I think back to the earliest days of his childhood. A happy baby, always smiling, rarely upset about anything, the largest blue eyes. As a toddler, happy go lucky, nary a care in the world, protected, safe and comfortable. In his youth an easy demeanor with a desire more apt in pleasing others and resolving conflict, than to be confrontational. As an adolescent, encouraging to others, artistically talented and establishing his confidence and the man he would become through the martial arts. Raised in a Christian home and taught to love the Lord and always seek His guidance in life.

Along the way Matthew made his share of mistakes, by no means was he perfect. Yet, one thing he learned early on in life was to always own up to his mistakes. When he first came to his father and I in 2003 to tell us he had decided to join the military, it was very difficult to comprehend, especially given that our nation was at war. We debated with him, but in the end knew we had to allow him the opportunity to make his own decision, even though there was a risk to doing so. And although we prayed, as did so many, for his safety, in the end it wasn't enough to spare him. From the day of his birth his life was in God's hands, and in the end I have to know He needed Matthew home with Him more than we needed him here with us.

Many have argued the wretchedness and stupidity of why man can't live in peace. Our men and women, often the very best and brightest our nation has raised are pledging their lives, their fortunes and their sacred honor for something they believe in. There are those who would argue whether they truly know what they are fighting or dying for. Knowing what I know from the discussions we had with Matthew, he understood what he was fighting for; simply said FREEDOM; a freedom those who feel so protected will never completely understand.

Over the past several years John and I have been asked to attend many events. Each intended to extend the gratitude of a community, a city, a state and even a nation for the sacrifice our son gave. Each time we attend such events we're humbled by the recognition and at times in awe of the very need for others to remember — to honor — to express their complete thanks for men and women like Matthew. If others are being recognized, we'll always take the time to look at the pictures of their heroes and heroines, and in so many we see Matthew. Each one of them has that same look in their eyes, each cut from the same whole cloth. These children became the men and women a parent always hoped and prayed they would be, and the ceremonies to remember them are fitting tributes to them and more importantly for their loved ones.

As we've walked this journey I've come to understand that my faith is the one value of absolute truth I have remaining. There are still days that pass when anger and bitterness overcome my thoughts and other times when I've found it difficult to forgive. But what I've come to terms with is that when everything is going just the way I want, faith is not true faith at all. Rather, when we encounter an event in our lives that shakes the foundation of our comfort and completely brings us to our knees, that is when faith becomes true; it becomes so very real! It's that real faith that has helped me to forgive, although I will never forget.

When a parent loses a child and especially their only child, it draws out the deepest of emotions. Emotions that at times have made it difficult for me to completely desire to pardon those who took our son's life. But, I know that one day they too will stand before a just and almighty God! Over time I have learned to let go of my anger, to nail it to the cross and to allow the Lord to heal the hole in my heart. It's fair to say that my faith took a deep bruising on November 15, 2005. But I have also come to know that it is that same faith that has held John and me together, and that continues to restore our hearts — to help us to trust again — to pick up the shattered pieces of our lives and to press on.

By pressing on we're able to touch the lives of so many others. As of this writing more than 2,000 families have benefited from the passage of The Holley Provision, a legacy left in honor of a young man who chose to step out and touch the lives of so many.

As I've met other wives and mothers I've spent time learning how they've walked this journey and gleaned insights from them. For me the pendulum of emotions over the past many years has swung from one extreme to the other. For several years I wracked my brain seeking the answer of why this had happened to us, an answer that I've come to accept I'll never know this side of heaven. In the first year I sheltered myself from so much because all I wanted to do was hide from the world. The company that I worked for at the time came to an equitable agreement with me that allowed me to take the next eight months off to focus on my emotional health.

There were so many friends, both those who had known us for years before Matthew's death, and those we've come to know these past five years, coupled with family members who embraced both John and me in love and prayer, who shed tears with us and when they didn't know what to say, simply sat and listened.

I sought answers in books written by other mothers who had suffered from the death of a child. My hope was to better understand how they had learned to cope with their pain. I attended grief counseling sessions through church. I struggled with questions about my faith; a faith that I wanted to be humble and obedient to, but to be honest I found myself carrying that burden of bitterness. It was only over this past year that I've started to come to terms with those things I have absolutely no control over, and as I have the questions of why, have changed to a simpler question for what purpose?

In my heart I know that it is God's grace that has led us through this storm in our lives. The life we knew before November 2005 has changed in so many ways and literally with each breath we take. I've learned to let go of what's gone and to take my sorrow to God before all else and to seek the comfort only He can provide both John and me. Another source of solace for me has been in my writing and sharing my heart with others. In years past writing was something I thought I was good at. I never felt comfortable putting myself out there, and so often times I would simply write to myself. On this journey as I've opened up I've found that sharing through my written word has inspired and encouraged others in so many ways. The following is a poem I wrote as we neared the one-year mark after Matthew's death, appropriately titled...

Hope

A year gone and many have mourned
A year gone and many have hope
Hope for a better tomorrow
Hope for far less sorrow

Where would we be if not for our faith?
A gracious God who gives us such strength
We grow stronger with each day
No debt for us to repay

For our family, the ultimate sacrifice given
From one well liked, bigger than life, driven
To serve a cause greater than he
To serve those who can only wish to be

For all a good son, loyal friend, a partner and companion
A strong heart and will, a soft heart and voice
A helping hand and a firm resolve
A believer in his Lord, and all that is good

This coming year, be willing to forgive
To love, laugh and to live
To know the gifts we have are from above
To share, to help and to be strong in our love

Hope for a better tomorrow
Hope for far less sorrow
Hope fills our heart
Hope for today, beyond and now we start...

I've come to accept that while there will always be evil in this world, there is far more love to go around and to be shared. In the end the only thing worth living for is to pass on that gift to those whose paths we're blessed to cross. Strength, honor and love for our Lord and for our son!

Afterwords

Celebrating Life

AS PARENTS IT SHOULD BE EASY for us to share the man — the soul who is our son. Some can go a lifetime wondering if they touched the lives of others. Yet the greatest tribute a friend can give another is to honor the impact that friend has had on their life.

The following pieces were shared at different points in time and reflect the essence of who Matthew John Holley was to his friends, and even strangers who have become friends. In his short twenty-one years he personified the spirit of a person far beyond his time. A person who loved life, loved his Lord and most of all, loved others.

SPC. Shawn Farrow, Combat Medic 1/320 Field Artillery 101st Division
Eulogy given November 2005 — Taji, Iraq

"Matthew Holley was a great friend to me and a valuable asset to Alpha team 1/320th field artillery battalion. At the time of his death I had known Matthew for just about a year and during that time he had become one of my closest friends.

"If I have learned anything from Matt's life it was the lesson of love. Matthew taught me how to look at a person from the inside out not just from their outer appearance. He had so much insight on the value of the human soul. The love that he had towards people, even his enemies, was unlike anything I have ever seen in another person in my short life. When there was someone in trouble he was always there to help. The devotion he had towards his gun line was a personal obligation to do his job to the best of his ability no matter what was happening in his life.

"There was a point when Matthew could have easily gotten out of the Army because of a personal ailment. But because of the love he had for those in this battalion he chose to leave his family and friends for his Soldiers. Matt had a true medic's mentality that it wasn't about him, rather it was about those he was charged with taking care of.

"Whenever I had challenges, Matt was always there for me to talk to. I could talk with him about anything, whether it was relationship problems, problems with the Army, or anything that I needed. He was always there! He always seemed to have the right answer for me when I needed it the most. Of all the problems I've had in my life he had so much knowledge about everything that he would always be able to help me find the right answer. Matt always had a way of telling things like they were; he never held back on anything he had to say. This characteristic often got him into trouble, but that is the trait that I most admired about him. No matter what the circumstances may have been he would always let you know how he felt about you.

"Recently I received an email from Matt's fiancée in which she shared that over 200 people came to her house to pay their respects after learning of his death. That means that Matthew touched the lives of over 200 others through his loss. I cannot even begin to explain the devotion he had for his fiancée. She was his life. She meant more to him in this world than anything. The only thing that he possibly cared about more was taking care of his Soldiers. He could not let them down! Matt died for his country honorably, yet the memories of his life have already and will continue to touch the lives of many people.

"It's difficult to explain the effect that Matt had on others, even after spending just a short period of time with them. He was the type of person that accepted everyone as they were because he understood them. Matt chose to be in this Army and knew the responsibility it entailed. He was the type of medic that couldn't be stuck back in the clinic working. He had to be on the line doing his job.

"I cannot explain how much I miss my friend. I just wish he was here to see how many people truly care about him. I know that he is in a much better place now and I have no need to worry, but I guess this is my chance to say goodbye.

"I love you Matt and I will never forget you! You are the type of person that no one could easily forget. One day I will be able to see you in Heaven my friend and then we will celebrate together.

"Goodbye Matt."

Jeff Edwards, Columnist at A View From the Deck Plate and Award-Winning Author of *TORPEDO* and *THE SEVENTH ANGEL*

Of Fathers and Sons

"John Holley and I lost our sons under completely different circumstances. My son, Joshua, died after a prolonged battle with bone cancer. John's son, Matthew, was killed by a roadside bomb in Iraq. We lost Josh a few weeks before his eighteenth birthday. Matt Holley was twenty-one years old. Matthew died in combat. Joshua passed away in his own bed. My family had nearly two years to prepare emotionally for the end of Josh's life. John and Stacey Holley's only warning was the unexpected ring of a doorbell and the arrival of uniformed strangers at their front door.

"I wrote a column about the Holley family at the beginning of 2006, just a few weeks after Matthew's death. John and Stacey were still oscillating between pride in Matthew's service and the extraordinary trauma of his loss, when they received some disturbing news about the military's plans for returning their son's remains. Matthew's body was being shipped to San Diego as freight on a commercial airliner. A Soldier would fly in the passenger cabin to act as escort for the body, but there would not be a military honor guard at Lindbergh Field. There would be no ceremony to mark the return of a fallen Soldier to the soil of his country. John and Stacey wouldn't even be allowed to meet their son's remains on the runway. They were told that they could claim his casket from the holding area for oversized luggage, after the suitcases and the rest of the freight had been offloaded from the plane.

"The arrangements for Matthew's return did not sit well with the Holleys, but they were even more disturbed to learn that this sort of handling was standard practice. Honors and ceremonies for deceased service members were rendered later, at the memorial service and funeral. The pre-funeral logistics followed procedures governing the transportation of commercial freight.

"In all fairness to the Army, I must note that there was a legitimate argument to be made for using commercial freight to ship military remains. It's often the quickest means of transportation available, and all branches of the U.S. military go to great effort to return fallen service members to their loved ones as quickly as possible. But for many grieving families, the dispassionate mechanics of the commercial freight process far outweighed the

benefits of speedy transportation. John Holley made this unmistakably clear during our very first phone conversation.

"I appreciate the desire to move quickly," John said. "It's good to know that people are working so hard to bring Matt home to us as soon as possible. But speed isn't the only consideration. What if the fastest transportation available was a garbage truck? Would they deliver my son's remains in that?"

"John was understandably upset when he asked me that question, and he chose a deliberately-exaggerated illustration to bring home his point. But stripped of emotion and hyperbole, I think his position was valid. When dealing with families that have been shattered emotionally, speed of service cannot be the only driving factor.

"John and Stacey Holley are both Army veterans themselves, and they tend to meet challenges head-on. Faced with a situation that compounded their family's grief, they decided to do something about it. With the assistance of the Casualty Assistance Office assigned to their family, they made contact with California Senator Barbara Boxer, who began making some telephone calls on their behalf. Senator Boxer had no trouble overriding bureaucratic obstacles that might have been insurmountable to the Holley family. John and Stacey were allowed to meet Matthew's casket on the runway at Lindbergh Field. A small military honor guard joined them in welcoming their son back to American soil. And that was all they'd really wanted — not streaming banners and marching bands — just the opportunity to offer their fallen Soldier some of the respect he had earned.

"In the weeks and months after Matt's funeral, the Holleys worked with Congressman Duncan Hunter, who was then Chairman of the House Armed Services Committee, to draft legislation governing the return of deceased military personnel to American soil. The resulting bill, "Transportation of Remains of Casualties Dying in a Theater of Combat Operations," was passed by Congress and as Section 563 of the Fiscal Year 2007 National Defense Authorization Act. This piece of landmark legislation, which President Bush signed into law in October 2006, became known as "The Holley Provision," in honor of Matthew Holley.

"The language of the law specifies that the remains of military personnel who die in a theater of combat be transported to the military airfield nearest to the intended place of internment, and

that a military escort be present at the arrival airfield to remove the remains from the aircraft and to render proper military honors. The law also allows next-of-kin to waive this requirement and accept transportation of the remains to the nearest commercial airport without delay. In my opinion, it's a good and necessary law, and one that was too long in coming.

"John Holley and I met face-to-face for the first time in August of 2006. We had spoken several times on the phone after our initial telephone interview, but we had never gotten around to meeting in person.

"My emotional connection to John's story was that of an American citizen and a former military man. As a guy who spent most of his adult life in uniform, I was frankly angered by the impersonal process currently used to repatriate the remains of our honored dead. As an American, I was shamed by our nation's failure to properly respect the sacrifices of the men and women who have laid down their lives in its defense. But when I met John Holley in person, I discovered a third emotional connection to this issue: that of a father who has lost a son.

"We must have been quite a sight — two grizzled old veterans sitting at a little round table under a shade umbrella in front of a coffee shop, crying our eyes out. I'm sure the other customers were appalled by our little spectacle, but I didn't care and I'm fairly certain that John Holley didn't care either.

"Neither of us had counted on turning our meeting into a tear-fest. We had planned to shake hands, drink a little coffee, and catch up on the progress toward "The Holley Provision." We did some of that, but mostly we talked about our sons. We dragged out photos of Josh and Matt, swapped favorite stories about our sons, and we cried — probably a lot more than middle aged men are supposed to cry.

"As I mentioned in the opening sentences of this column, the deaths of Matthew Holley and Joshua Edwards did not have much in common. Their lives, by contrast, were similar enough to give me chills. Matt was a three-time AAU national karate champion, and Josh had a wall full of medals for Kung Fu. They were both gifted amateur artists. They listened to the same music. They watched the same Japanese anime cartoons. Matthew was in the Army. Joshua was Junior Army ROTC, and looking forward to enlisting after high

school. And when John and I compared photos, we discovered that our sons looked enough alike to be brothers.

"It was this last bit, I think, that caused me to abandon all pretense of courage and break down into tears. Because Matt and Josh could have been brothers. I could see myself sitting in John Holley's chair on the opposite side of that coffee shop table. For a few seconds, I could feel the pain of his loss as keenly as I feel the loss of Joshua. And my heart was broken all over again.

"This nation can never repay the debt that it owes to John and Stacey Holley, or to the other American families struggling with the loss of their fallen warriors. But we can help these families face the unthinkable with a little more dignity. We can demonstrate our respect and our gratitude for their sacrifice by allowing them to welcome their loved ones home in a manner befitting heroes.

"It undoubtedly takes more effort to transport our honored dead as heroes, and it certainly costs more money than the existing commercial freight mechanism. But those expenses are insignificant compared to the price paid by our warriors and their families. And if the most powerful and prosperous nation on earth cannot be troubled to render this small honor to its defenders, then maybe we've forgotten what we were fighting for in the first place."

SPC Matthew J. Holley
by Natalie Johnsen — November 15, 2010

"It's been five years today since Matthew Holley was taken from everyone that loved him and that he loved. He was a son, a best friend and he acted like a brother to so many of us. He was always protective of me and everyone he cared about. That was just one of those amazing qualities that Matt had. Was Matt perfect? Of course not, but that doesn't mean that he wasn't a great person. Matt, I love you and miss you and I've been thinking about you so much all week. All of the memories that we had growing up together...

*"Do you remember when we wanted to watch **Sleepy Hollow**? My Mom didn't want me to watch it, but for some reason you and I still thought it would be a good idea to just watch it in the living room like we would never get caught. LOL my Mom was not happy about that one — ha-ha — sorry Mom!*

*"You always made me watch Kung Fu movies! Man you loved those movies and trying the "cool moves" with me as you liked to call them and I would always end up with bruises ha-ha. We would watch **Crouching Tiger, Hidden Dragon** and **Kill Bill 1&2**. I now own those movies because they remind me of you!*

We always ended up going with our Moms while they shopped or whatever they were doing, and every time we were on the beach you would pick up seashells for me because you knew how much I loved them. I will never forget when you found a whole sand dollar! You were SO excited about it.

"I will never forget the night my parents came home and told me what happened... I arrived home around nine, and my parents were not home. I got kind of worried that something had happened to them cause let's face it, parents should be home by nine! So I sat down in the chair to watch TV and wait for them. They came home and woke me up at around one in the morning and I knew right away that something was wrong by the look on their faces. I will never forget my Mom looking at me and trying not to cry. As long as I live I will never forget what she said — she looked at me and said Matt was killed and went home to be with the Lord and I looked between my mom and my dad and finally whispered — 'Please tell me you're kidding.'

"I remember going to work the next day and just stayed in the kitchen the whole day and washed dishes because if anyone looked at me I would burst into tears again. I think everyone I worked with was too scared to even talk to me. That whole week was a complete blur and I don't really remember it at all.

"The day before we left for your funeral my dad and I got a cold and I was so drugged up on cold medication that not only was I in a daze because I couldn't believe that you were actually gone, but with the cold meds, I was kind of out of it. I don't think I said a lot the first day I was there. I remember staring at your casket with the flag draped over it and all I could think of was that you couldn't really be in there and that someone was just going to jump up and yell "just joking!" But... that never happened. For some reason Zaphea and I connected right away. I don't think I could have made it through both services without her. Poor Pablo had to pretty much make me write down my email so we could stay in touch because I was still pretty out of it with the whole stupid cold thing.

"All these years later I still miss you Matt! So much! I wish that this had never happened. So many good things have happened since. God has used your death in such a great way — letting your parent's touch so many lives. Even so that doesn't take away the fact that I still wish you could be here. But just know that I love you very much and miss you even more. You were an amazing friend Matt and you will never be forgotten!

"Much love,

"Me"

Behind the Title

<u>Stacey</u>:

John thought of the title *Medals, Flags and Memories* shortly after Matthew's funeral services had concluded. He was trying to come up with the words for a song that would honor Matthew and the sacrifice he and his fellow Soldiers had made. John's inspiration for the title came from the song "Poems, Prayers and Promises" by John Denver. After reflecting on the events that had occurred in the short few weeks following Matthew's death, the words in the title represented three elements of the military honors service that every Fallen American Hero receives. The elements are:

Medals — representing the awarding of the medals to the parents or spouse for their heroes service.

Flags — representing the folded flag that draped the casket and was given to the loved ones on behalf of a grateful nation.

Memories — represents what the family is left with — the good, with the bad; the finality of it all.

The following is a beautiful poem that Stacey wrote after being inspired by the title:

Medals, Flags and Memories

When all is said and done, the services are complete and you're left to self, what is there?
Tears - plenty, more than you ever thought were possible
Anguish - pain beyond belief, gut wrenching, heart piercing, life scarring
Questions - many more than most could comprehend.
Answers - few, especially in the beginning, than you begin to pick-up the shattered pieces,
and the answers come slowly

Medals presented in honor, on behalf of a grateful nation
There is meaning behind each, some going as far back as the Revolutionary War
A Purple Heart, awarded in the name of the President of the United States
Given to those who have been wounded or killed while serving our great nation
The Bronze Star, The Silver Star, Distinguished Service Medals, Crosses, perhaps A Medal of Honor
Medals awarded to those who distinguished themselves by heroic or meritorious achievement
Extraordinary heroes who at the risk of their own lives, went above and beyond in the call of duty
Campaign medals highlight the appreciation of a grateful country to the sacrifices made

Flags, many more than you thought you could hold
Oh the power in a folded flag, what symbolism, strength, and honor
All of us would trade them to have our loved ones back
To see their smiles, their passion, their conviction and yes their heart
For you and I, for their fellow man

And, then the memories flood... Initially with the greatest of pain, this is said to heal over time

Memories of happy times, youth, aspirations for life, and for those they
would come to influence
Maybe they were sisters or brothers, husbands or wives, a mother or
father, a cousin, aunt or uncle or even grandparents

From many walks of life, many cultures, many ambitions, all tied to a
common bond "To Protect and Defend"
Our days are taken up wondering, praying and hoping
No one wishes for war, no one desires the hurt and pain that
accompanies
We can only pray that another doesn't hear that dreadful knock on the
door,
That statement "We regret to inform you"

In the end it is the Medals, Flags and Memories that remain;
How poignant if only we had known
If we could, would we have tried to change the path?
Could we have changed the path?
Questions to ponder, all for a grateful nation...

Matthew John Holley, November 1992

Made in the USA
Charleston, SC
21 June 2011